# Information Graphic

INNOVATIVE SOLUTIONS IN CONTEMPORARY DESIGN

D0517488

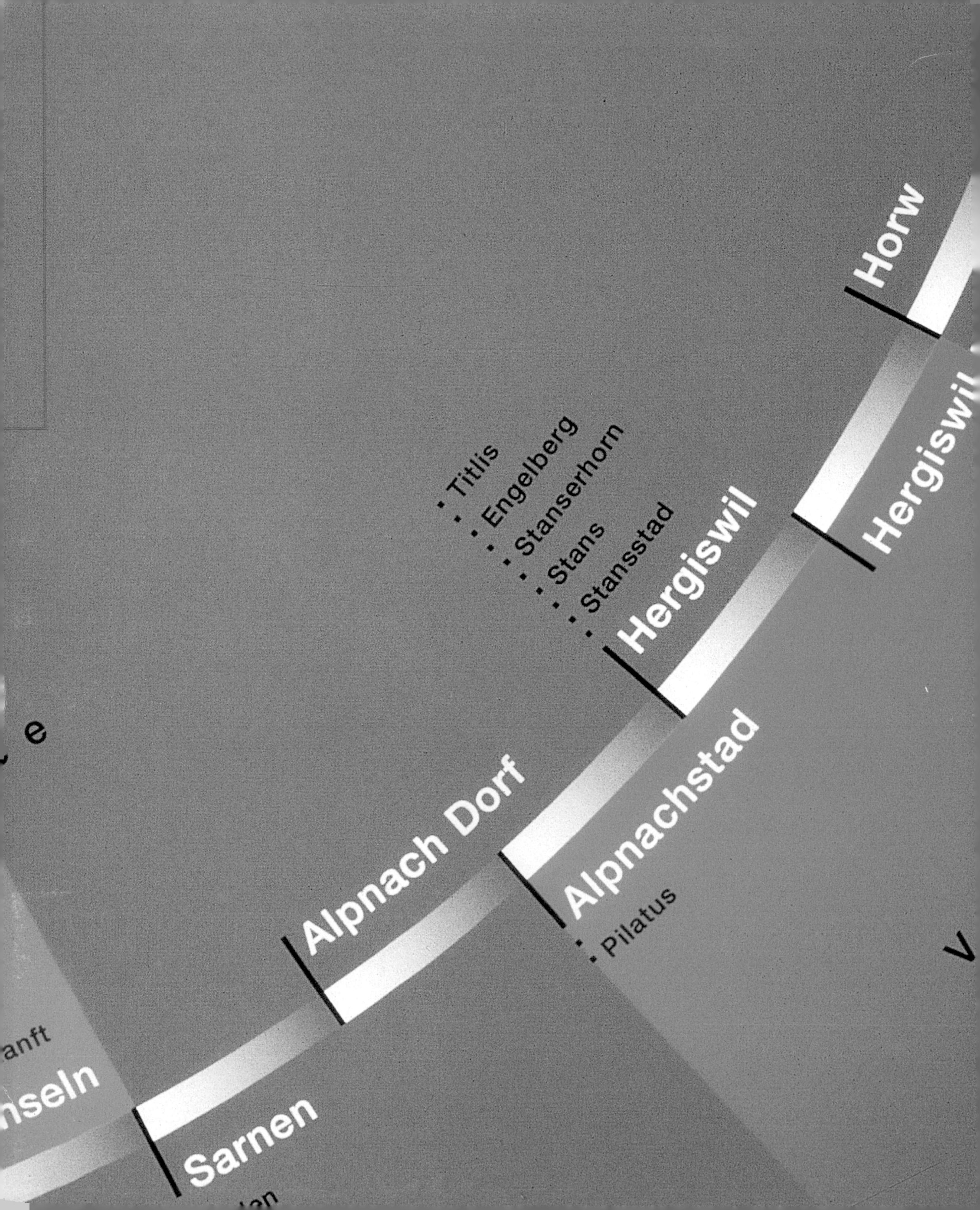

Horw

Hergiswil

Hergiswil

Titlis
Engelberg
Stanserhorn
Stans
Stansstad

Alpnach Dorf

Alpnachstad

Pilatus

e

nseln

anft

Sarnen

V

# Information Graphics

## INNOVATIVE SOLUTIONS IN CONTEMPORARY DESIGN

PETER WILDBUR AND MICHAEL BURKE

With 300 color illustrations

Thames and Hudson

Design © 1998 Thames and Hudson Ltd, London
Texts © 1998 Peter Wildbur and Michael Burke

First published in hardcover in the United States of America in 1998 by
Thames and Hudson Inc., 500 Fifth Avenue, New York, New York 10110

First paperback edition 1999

Library of Congress Catalog Card Number 98-60235

ISBN 0-500-28077-0

Printed in Hong Kong

**Title Page** Detail of Swiss National Railways
Scenic Route Indicator, designed by Sandra Hoffmann
of Stahli-Hoffmann (see p. 40)

# Contents

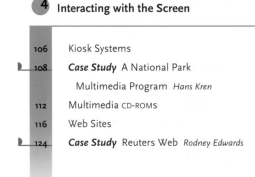

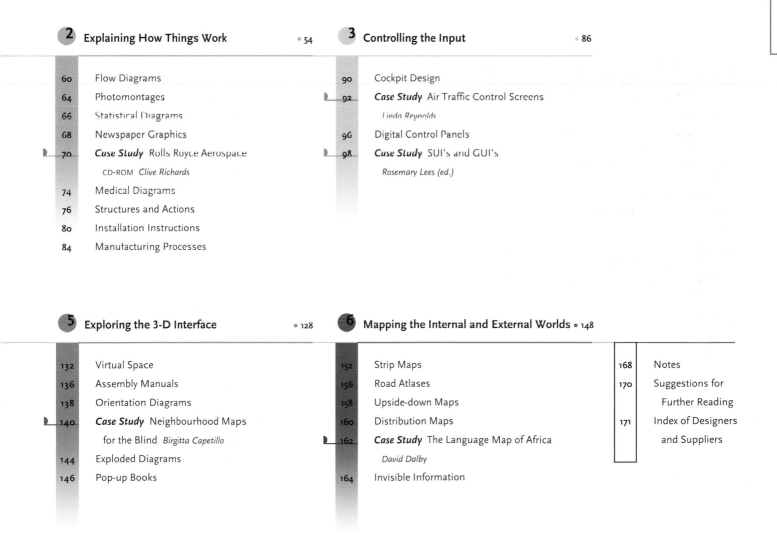

# Introduction

The Information Designer's Role

Information design in its widest sense is about the selection, organization and presentation of information to a given audience. Information itself can come from almost any source – a weather map, a timetable listing flight departures or a pile of statistical data. In some areas of information design, the content can be vast – as, for example, in a map – and the user extracts only what is needed for a particular purpose. In other cases, the content may lie not so much in the information itself as in its movement in a given direction or even in its rate of change.

Information design as a discipline has the efficient communication of information as its primary task, and this implies a responsibility that the content be both accurate and unbiased in its presentation. Unlike much of advertising and marketing design, in which the object is to persuade the user into a course of action,

information design tries to present all the objective data required to enable the user to make some kind of decision. Information is usually only of value to us if it includes material we are not already aware of. The idea that information already known to us is not taken in by the brain was expressed very simply by the anthropologist-philosopher Gregory Bateson in 1979, when he offered a definition of information as 'Any difference which makes a difference'. Although Bateson was writing about the purely technical details of transmitting information signals within an electronic system, his statement nonetheless applies to the way in which our brains either accept or reject information in general.

The information designer has been described as a 'transformer' of information – whether of raw data, a set of actions or a process – into a visual model capable of revealing its essence in terms

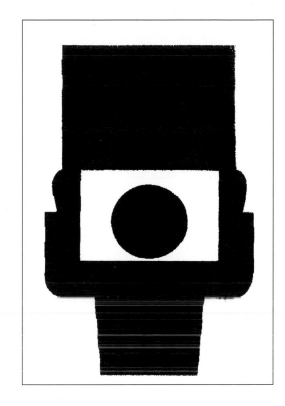

1

ISOTYPE **Logo**

This is the logotype of the ISOTYPE Institute of Vienna; it dates from about 1928.

which a particular audience can grasp easily. The term 'transformer' was adopted by Otto Neurath, the Austrian philosopher and social scientist and founder of ISOTYPE (International System of Typographical Picture Education) [1]. Practising in the 1920s and '30s, Neurath saw designers as intermediaries between historians, economists and mathematicians and their audiences [2].

Most of the work illustrated in this book falls into one of three general categories. The first involves information presented as an organized arrangement of facts or data, such as a timetable, a signing system and most maps, from which users are free to extract only that information which they need for a given purpose. The second involves information presented as a means of understanding a situation or process, such as a guide-book, a bar-chart or a stage-by-stage description of how to get a machine to operate. The third category involves the design of control systems, such as that of input and feedback controls of a product or vehicle.

> *Excellence consists of complex ideas communicated with clarity, precision, and efficiency and that is just as true of the new media as of the old.*
>
> Edward R. Tufte

### Technological change

Throughout history, changes in technology have influenced the way in which designers have gone about their work. Hardware has evolved slowly and has usually been modified or created by people intimately connected with the technology being superseded. If we think, for example, of the transformation in typesetting from the advent of metal type (used for several hundred years) to film

**Instructions for Telephoning**

This example of non-verbal communication was illustrated in the 1936 English edition of *International Picture Language* by Otto Neurath. It was seen as a model for an international visual language for instructions, in this case, the procedure for using the telephone. The simplified graphic approach has an almost timeless quality which would be difficult to improve upon.

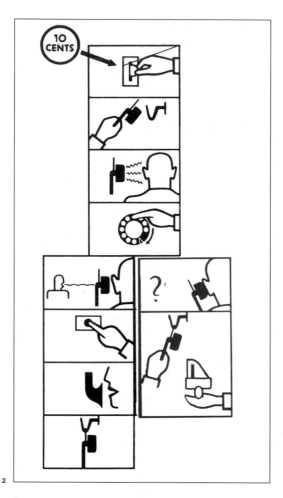

2

quaint term) transformed the time-honoured system completely and in a relatively short time. Designers found themselves in direct control of machines and having to wear a number of hats in order to stay in business. Most information designers made the transition and now welcome their total control over the process of initiating screen- or print-based material.

In the beginning, the design of computers and early software was aimed at the business market and focused on accounting and word processing. Only when these markets had been covered did software publishers look around for new fields to conquer. It was almost by accident that the graphic arts came to be seen as a new market for which the manipulation of type-faces, images and page make-up held out enormously exciting possiblities. For the first time in several hundred years, the tools used by designers and typographers were modified without their direct participation. Consequently, designers in particular found the early graphics programs to be extremely primitive. Most of these shortcomings have been overcome, however, and today we have a situation in which almost any design or typographic requirement can be satisfied.

In addition to the disappearance of the 'expert' who acted as a buffer between designer and machine, a whole range of changes were associated with the digital revolution. First was the use of the computer monitor, the screen of which became the centre of the designer's creative focus, uniting previously diverse inputs on to a single surface. Word processing, type, images and, more recently, video could be manipulated with the same tools and in the same context and transmitted in a single digital medium. Above all, the new technology provided 'quantity', whether of data or of type-faces. Choices were almost unlimited and were enlarging continually. Digital technology also

setting and then, fairly rapidly, to early forms of digital typesetting, the actual setting skills remained in the hands of trained 'compositors', craftsmen who served a long trade apprenticeship and who acted as intermediaries between designers and machines. The designer's role was that of specifier, and his or her relationship to the compositor was rather like that between an architect and a builder. Most of the ancillary roles in the printing industry were performed by other specialists – proof-readers, photographic retouchers, artworkers and reproduction specialists.

The advent of personal computers changed all this. Desktop publishing (now seen as rather a

meant speed of access, of modification of elements and of transmission of final results to end users. The other important dimension to digital technology was the introduction of the concept of 'interactivity', which enabled the user to make choices, to follow his or her own path through a program or text. Based on a feature known as hypertext, interactivity became the basis for the development of multimedia and the Internet and, in the commercial sphere, made on-screen shopping a reality.

It is probably pointless to single out particular programs for discussion here since obsolescence is built in to software design. The specific requirements of designers and typographers are being catered for with increasing success and efficiency, and even though the user base may be relatively small, specialist programs are continually being produced or modified. There has been a steady convergence of the complicated early MS-DOS command systems and the image-based 'icon' approach of the Apple Macintosh system. Not that all users believe this to be a good thing. In her well-documented book *Life on the Screen: Identity in the Age of the Internet,* Sherry Turkle compares the users of commands, who have a strong belief in the 'transparency' of the system, in having direct control of the inner workings of the machine, with the users of the Macintosh icon-based system. She likens the control-system users to the owners of vintage cars, for whom the sound and feel of the controls take precedence over the information shown on the car's dials and who have direct access to the inner workings of the engine by simply undoing the bonnet. Macintosh users, on the other hand, like many modern drivers, rely on the interface of dials and warning lights and may never look under the bonnet of their new automobiles.

### Analogue or numerical?

This divergence may have something in common with that between the proponents of numerical and analogue methods of presenting information. The argument between these modes can be illustrated most simply by considering the design of clock and watch faces over the past twenty years. The traditional clock face uses an *analogue* method of showing time by means of moving hands sweeping around a calibrated dial. In a similar

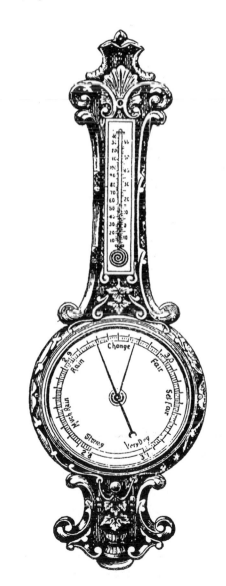

3

**Traditional Barometer**

This traditional barometer features the analogue (dial) presentation of information about atmospheric pressure.

### Decimal Time

This is an analogue clock face with a difference. It is calibrated for Decimal Time, a system invented by Michael Pinder, President of the Decimal Time Society. Pinder has described his system as follows: 'Scientific time, based upon an arbitrary second of fixed duration and measured by an atomic clock, is already decimalized. Civil time is variable, based upon astronomical observations and uses traditional units. This Decimal Time system proposed by me will begin at midnight in Greenwich on the vernal equinox in 2000 AD. At that moment a digital timepiece will read 000:000.00 giving age:date.time. An analogue timepiece will have ten divisions. It can show the day number in the ten-day week as well as the time of day and can also indicate when it will get light or dark … The year will be 36 weeks plus a remainder of 5 or 6 days. These will be reserved for local, regional, national and international elections in a four-year cycle.' This illustration comes from Pinder's *Time on Our Hands*.

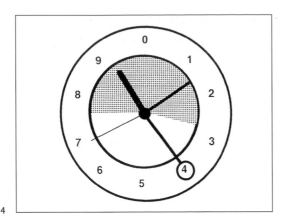

4

### Digital Barometer

Besides displaying pressure, this digital barometer shows the temperature and humidity, all with a choice of units. It is of interest for its combination of a numerical presentation of the above plus an analogue (bar-chart) display of pressure readings stored for the previous twenty-four hours and a simple pictographic treatment for the predicted weather.

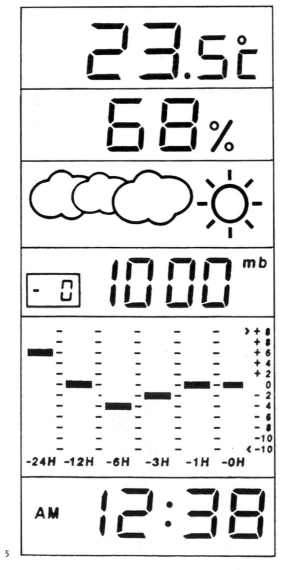

5

manner, the traditional aneroid barometer [3] shows atmospheric pressure by means of a single hand on a dial which is often inscribed with the words 'stormy', 'change', 'set fair' and so on (the words also acting in an analogue way). The *numerical* displays of clocks, watches and barometers present the same information as a digital readout. In both conceptual and practical terms, digital presentation could not be more different from earlier forms of analogue time displays such as the sundial, which used a moving shadow to indicate the passing of time, or, from an even earlier period, the sand in an hour glass.

What all of these analogue instruments have in common is a frame of reference or context in which one is able to place the 'present' moment [4]. In the case of the traditional clock, we relate the present moment to the larger framework of before or after noon, to the context of the present hour and, finally, to a particular five-minute span. This sense of context is in some way very satisfying, perhaps because it accords with the way in which we normally sense and observe things, relating the particular to the general, whether consciously or unconsciously. This is a mode in which the context is always stated or at least implied. Broadly speaking, the analogue mode of presentation encodes a graphic context along with the information itself, thus enabling the viewer both to grasp the significance of the message and to place it within recognizable parameters.

Today's digital technology has made it possible to incorporate analogue and numerical modes into a single product display [5], thus gaining the advantages of both formats. This duality of presentational formats applies equally to information presented as printed matter or on screen. In the case of statistical material, there can be no doubt as to the speed of assimilation when raw figures are presented in an analogue graphic form such as an isotype chart, bar-chart or pie diagram. Numerical presentation, on the other hand, provides the user with the greatest precision and can be shown to as many decimal places as required. Perhaps its greatest weakness is that rapid changes in information can make it difficult to assess both direction and rate of change, a factor which can have important safety implications in the case of, say, an aircraft's altimeter.

Increasingly, digital and analogue are being employed together to provide both contextual and numerically precise information. One of the great design challenges is to find ways of graphically integrating these complementary modes of communication into a seamless whole.

### *Statistical formats*

The basic requirement for any statistical presentation is the existence of reasonably accurate figures over a period of time. This type of information became available in Europe, mainly from government sources, from the middle of the eighteenth century. The earliest forms of statistical diagrams were invented and developed later in that century, most notably by J. H. Lambert (1728–1777),

**Booth's Map of London**

An extensive research project published in 1889 which covered the whole of London, the complete text ran to seventeen volumes, each of which contained litho-printed fold-out map sections. There was one master map using hand-coloured annotation from which this illustration is taken; it shows the Paddington area of west London. For the colour key, see page 150. *Courtesy the Museum of London*

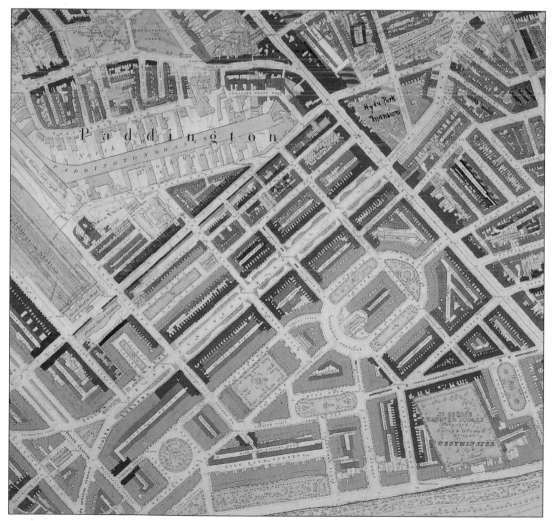

a Swiss-German mathematician, and William Playfair (1759–1823), an English political economist.

Playfair introduced the time-series graph, bar-charts, pie charts and the variable-area diagram in a series of illustrations published mainly in two books, *The Commercial and Political Atlas* of 1786 and *The Statistical Breviary* of fifteen years later. Although little known in this context, another signicant figure in the history of statistical diagrams is Florence Nightingale (1820–1910). Her pioneering work in the area of nursing reform owes much to the way in which she marshalled the statistics of the appalling casualties of the Crimean War. Nightingale was able to show that during the first months of the Crimean campaign, there was a mortality rate amongst the troops of sixty per cent from *disease* alone. She was one of the first to use, although she probably did not invent it, the polar-area diagram to dramatically emphasize her casualty figures. Since polar-area diagrams are made up of a series of segments radiating from a central point, Nightingale referred to them as 'coxcomb' diagrams. This was the origin of the

revolutionary notion that social phenomena could be objectively measured and graphically represented. A similar idea underlay the social documentation presented in Charles Booth's monumental cataloguing of London's poor (see [6], p. 150 [4]).

One of the best-known diagrams of this period is Charles Joseph Minard's 'Napoleon's March to Moscow'. In this graphic, Minard (1781–1870) imaginatively combined statistical information with a time-line treatment. His diagram plots a number of variables, showing the size of Napoleon's army during the advance on Moscow and its decimation during the retreat, its movement with reference to place names and, most tellingly, the freezing temperatures on various dates. The time-line diagram, or synchronoptic method, for plotting a wide range of social and educational events along a horizontal time base is the other enduring graphical form from this period. It was first used by Joseph Priestley (1733–1804), the English scientist and teacher, and by William Playfair and has remained popular as a format for charts and

**The Bayeux Tapestry**

The Bayeux Tapestry is a remarkable eleventh-century visual narrative of the events leading up to the Norman invasion of the Anglo-Saxon kingdom of Harold.
It measures 230 feet in length and twenty inches in width and contains Latin 'subtitles'. There are no clear divisions into separate scenes and the viewpoint is fixed, but we are given the simplest of visual clues to denote an interior scene, a woodland, a road or the English Channel.

7

encylopaedias for recording such diverse subjects as the history of commerce, lives of famous people and world speed records (see [9]).

An important but somewhat later landmark among graphic diagrams is the work of the previously mentioned Otto Neurath. The name of Neurath's International System of Typographical Picture Education hints at the social and educational aims which informed all of his Institute's work. The stylized pictorial treatment of isotype was designed to be understood by people irrespective of language or cultural background, a theme developed later by transportation authorities around the world through the use of pictograms. The principle at the heart of the isotype designs was the use of pictorial symbols, always of identical size, which represented fixed amounts of information and which could be repeated to denote larger quantities. The strength of the isotype approach was to give immediate graphic interest to statistical material without the need for detailed captions or explanations.

All of these graphic formats, developed within a half-century of one another, have been easily assimilated into digital media, often with the benefits of animation. In essence, they all attempt to make sense of often complex numerical material by showing it in a simple pattern or by contrasting events in instantly recognizable ways. Most importantly, the formats are remembered even after the specific information in them is forgotten.

> *We think in pictures. Picture is understood here not as a painted picture but as a frame with various contents that are perceptible and comparable simultaneously, and thus open to assessment … The crucial factor is the perception of various contents that can be compared, that create analogy, alongside each other.*
>
> Otl Aicher

### Time-based Information

Today's time-based media, ranging from film to multimedia, all have one thing in common: the difficulty of recreating them on the printed page. The nearest the print medium has come

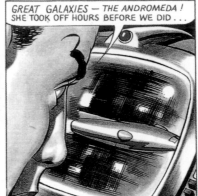

8

**Eagle Strip Cartoon**

This sequence from the 'Dan Dare' comic strip of the early 1960s shows most of the conventions of the genre: regular-depth frames with width dependent on story-line or setting, dialogue bubbles containing minimal text and contrasting 'camera' angles. Originally drawn by Frank Hampson, these strips were later produced by a team of artists.
*Dan Dare © 1998 Fleetway Editions. Reproduced courtesy of Hawk Books, U.K.*

to representing sequential movement is probably in the 'flickbooks' made by schoolchildren, but these are limited to a few seconds' 'playing' time.

Probably the best-known example of historical graphical reporting is the medieval Bayeux Tapestry [7], which depicts an unbroken sequence of events over a length of 230 feet. Possibly based on the principle of a scroll, a form of presentation in which the imagery is unrolled in front of the viewer, the tapestry presents its story in an ideal format, given a large enough venue for it to be displayed. The tapestry incorporates a form of Latin subtitling which is contained within the image area, and the top and bottom borders show associated events, such as the appearance of Halley's Comet (see p. 151 [5]).

Today, the essential tool for creating any time-based program is still the old-fashioned storyboard, which, while two-dimensional, enables a designer or director to plan a sequence of still or moving images regardless of duration or complexity. Storyboards as we know them were certainly used from the early days of film making, but are difficult to date since they rarely lasted much beyond the completion of a film. They provided a creative tool for visualizing a screenplay and also acted as a graphic indicator of camera angles, lighting effects and set design, as well as indicating details of sound and musical accompaniment.

Comic strips, related to the storyboard concept but graphic and narrative ends in themselves, evolved out of the political and satirical cartoons of

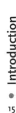

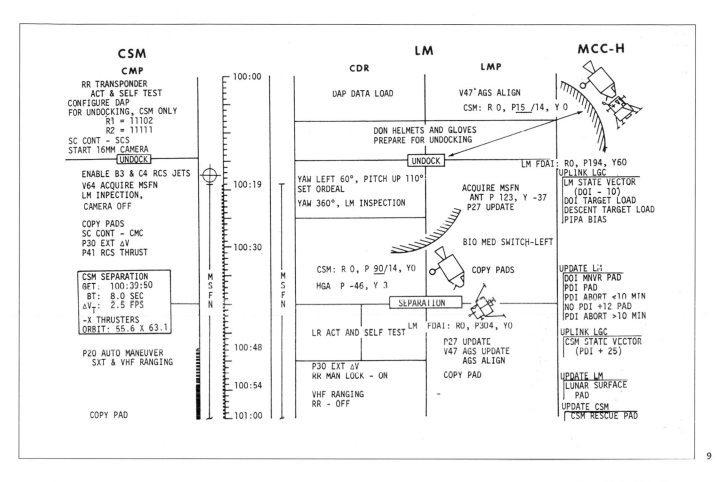

9

the eighteenth century. They were rapidly transformed from an adult medium into the primary format for children's comic papers. The storyboard in this form gradually developed a standard grid of regular 'frames' which were to be read from left to right and top to bottom. Descriptive text and dialogue were kept to an absolute minimum and usually set outside the frames so as not to interrupt the visual narrative. Later refinements were the conventions of 'dialogue' balloons and 'thought' bubbles; variable-width frames (long before the use of the wide screen in the cinema), and descriptive elements within the images to avoid the need for lengthy captioning [8].

The storyboard and comic-strip techniques have borrowed from each other, and both have been considerably enriched in the process. The attractiveness and compulsive nature of the storyboard format in its printed form has encouraged its use in a whole range of applications, from safety instructions of all kinds [10] to information and DIY manuals. As a working tool for the creation of moving images, it is still of primary importance for designers of everything from electronic games to multimedia programs, which fuse graphics, sound, music and digital video. Storyboard-based software programs such as Director allow the user to create a wide range of presentations, including business reports, vending and kiosk productions, CD-ROM titles and information for use on the Internet. A skilled user

**Moon Mission Flight Plan**

This is part of a flight-plan diagram from the 1969 Apollo 11 moon missions organized by NASA in the United States. Based on a time-line concept, it carries information as to when certain procedures should be carried out.

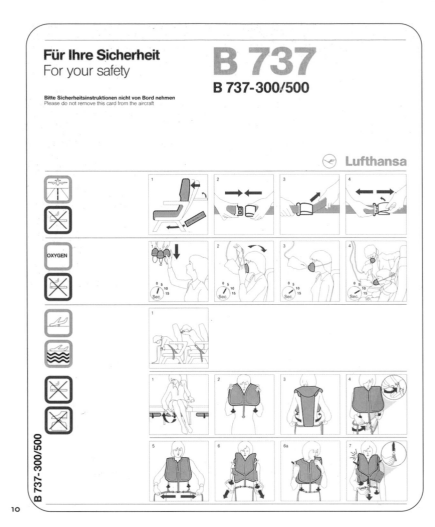

10

**Lufthansa 737 Safety Chart**

Lufthansa's safety chart uses
storyboard techniques to
show a sequence of events
and avoids captioning, which
would require translation into
a number of languages.
Having no text required very
careful planning, the use of
several colours and public
testing to avoid ambiguity.
(See p. 59 [9].)

can 'import' text, sound and animation using
built-in editors and then incorporate interactive
elements which can be synchronized over a
time base.

### The future

There can be little doubt that information design
will have a major role to play over the next ten
years. The sheer proliferation of factual information
from every media source looks certain to go on
increasing and will require ever more sophisticated
means of selection and filtering and more
structured presentations to make sense of it.

One area in which changes are imminent is
travel. The user of public transport, particularly of
bus and coach services, will have the same level
of information about destination, frequency and
arrival time as is currently available to airline
passengers, not only at departure points but at
each boarding point along a route. Terminals and
main stations will have electronic information
points, probably linked to the Internet, and will
be capable of providing comprehensive travel
information, including connections with other
forms of transport. Print-outs will be provided
of timetables and journey routes.

Drivers will also benefit from advances in
information design. On-board car navigation
systems will become part of a vehicle's standard
equipment, hopefully with the battle for formats
settled early on. It has long been predicted that
head-up displays, readable through a car's
windscreen, will come into general use, and this
may happen sooner than later due to action on
the part of the safety lobby. Personal navigation
systems will probably contain a screen display
switchable between three types of graphics:
alphabetical using a verbal/spoken description,
symbolic using arrows and pictograms,
or cartographic using a moving cursor on a
simplified map. Airline passengers are already
being provided with animated route information
[11], and it will not be long before travellers will be
able to see the flight-deck view of the landscape on
seat-back screens from anywhere in an aircraft.

Technological change is occurring so rapidly
that it would be pointless to try and predict
which system or program will lead the way in the
future. The general principle which seems to apply
to all types of technology, however, is that of
convenience: whichever system is most convenient
to the user will succeed above all others. If we think

of the struggles between sound-disc systems, photographic film formats or command versus icon systems, all have been won by the more convenient alternatives. Cost has been proven not to be a major factor.

As products get progressively more complex and have an increasing range of applications, it seems probable that explanatory matter will split into two main forms: on-screen instruction manuals on interactive discs for fixed products, and printed information for portable products. Printed instructions might be replaced by a yet-to-be-created hand-held liquid crystal display as thin as the present smart card but of A5–A4 size and capable of the short-duration playing of animated diagrammatic material. Such instruction displays with add-on programs could replace relatively bulky present-day laptop computers.

Statistical information is likely to develop new diagrammatic formats beyond those used at the present time. The graph, bar-chart and pie diagram plus a few other more specialized formats [12] have been invaluable tools for communicating statistical information, but it is almost certain that after a period of almost three hundred years new formats will be created, perhaps driven by the requirements of the moving image in interactive media.

All of this implies that design students of the future will need to have a much wider range of skills than most graphic and multimedia students possess today. The coming together of typography, graphics, the moving image, sound and music requires training in both aesthetic judgment and technical skills, as well as the ability to implement and commission multimedia productions. Such a program hardly exists today, and it may be that designers of the future will find themselves on courses equal in duration and related in structure to those followed by architects.

11

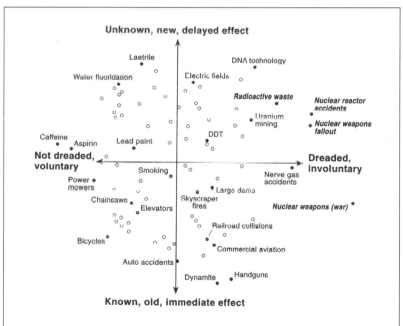

12

**In-flight Video Map**

One of a sequence of maps from the Flight Master 2000 video display.
*Design: Chapman Bounford & Associates, U.K.; client: Airborne Display Ltd, U.K.*

**Cognitive Map of Risk Perception**

While not a new format, this central-axis diagram presents statistical material in a completely new light. Reproduced from Mark Monmonier's 1997 book *Cartographies of Danger* and devised by Paul Slovic, the map is based on the views of laypeople asked to rate eight hazards on eighteen risk characteristics. For clarity, only twenty-six of the hazards are labelled here.

# Informing the Traveller

**Signing Systems • Building Identity • Digital Route-finding
Route Indicators • Route Maps • Public Transport Systems**

Pre-electronic aids for train passengers looking for travel information were based mainly on printed timetables in both poster and pocket-sized formats. Time and close attention were required to decipher these accurately. The seemingly intractable problem – still with us today – lay in making clear the bewildering number of exceptions to the listed services. These included variations for weekends and public holidays, ticketing limitations and many others.

The traditional timetable presented a classic problem of information overload that was only really solved with the introduction of electronic ticketing machines. In contrast, the indicator board has always been successful in giving airline passengers an unobstructed view of departure and arrival information on a scale which can be read across a concourse; the only recent improvement has been the change from mechanical flap

mechanisms to electronic ones. Railway passengers are beginning to enjoy some of these sophisticated electronic display signs. Digital technology has made it possible to make comprehensive departure and destination information available at regular intervals on every station platform to augment main-concourse departures and arrivals boards. The same technology is being used to provide information within each passenger coach. Being presented with this information visually rather than via audio announcements is much less disruptive for most passengers. At some point in the future, the same technology might provide information of local interest to tourists.

A related development, though not electronic in nature, is the installation in some Swiss National Railways carriages of scenic 'viewing platforms' similar to those often found at viewing points in the

1

countryside to identify distant landmarks. The railway versions consist of horizontal semi-circular diagrams which enable passengers to identify features such as lakes and mountains during their journey (pp. 40–41 [1–4]). The displays, which are placed adjacent to the windows on both sides of the carriages, have proven to be popular with passengers.

Recent work in the signing of complete transport systems such as bus networks (pp. 44–45 [1–8]), airports (pp. 22–23 [1–5]), marine centres (pp. 26–27 [1–5]) and pedestrian routes (p. 28 [1–2]) have concentrated on establishing strong corporate identities to link together the often widely scattered locations through which the passenger engages with the system. These are often linked visually with the corporate identity of the town or city itself. In the best of these schemes, great attention is paid to the detailed treatment of route

maps, destination boards and timetables.

The scale of international airports and the vast car-parking facilities associated with them has inspired planners and designers to provide the means to enable a driver in a remote car park to reach the correct terminal building, where a conventional sign system takes over. A map or

**London Bus Route Map**

This transport map, applied directly to the side of a London bus, supplements the destination panel on the front. The sequences of stops and final destination are clearly visible above most other traffic.

2

weather and night-time conditions, and the need for a series of advance 'prompt' signs to permit early lane changing. Increasingly, digital signs, with their capacity to rapidly change their messages to convey local information and hazards, are complementing static ones. At present, these are mainly of the dot-matrix type and are only capable of a low level of definition due to too few light-point sources. Thus they can provide a barely acceptable level of communication far below that of present-day static signing.

Digital technology has provided several important navigational aids for the driver, including the CD-ROM-based route-planning program (p. 36–37 [1–3]). Such programs may be adjusted according to the type of route required, which might favour speed, scenic interest or, say, towing a caravan. The user can also bring up details along the route of any one of a number of facilities such as hotels, petrol stations or historic sites. In fact, navigation systems for vehicles date from at least the 1950s. One hand-held mapping device was able to select and present to the driver a range of map sections covering a large part of the country by means of an ingenious system of map folding [2], while another utilized a mechanical drive from the car's gear box to scroll a map across a window in a small device situated close to the driver.

In the early days of computers, and long before satellite-positioning systems were invented, a number of navigation systems were produced which either made use of external transmitters and were thus limited to city use, or which made use of an on-board computer. One such system carried a database based on a series of map cassettes; the vehicle was equipped with sensors which detected changes to its direction and the distance travelled. This system was claimed to be extremely accurate, with the vehicle's position always remaining in the

### Automappa

This ingenious navigational aid probably dates from the late 1950s as the U.K.'s motorways are not included. The double-sided plastic housing contains a set of parallel-folded map sections which can be moved by means of side levers to reveal any one of a number of sections of the complete road network; the reverse shows the entire network.

route plan is printed out at the car-park ticket machine, and each machine provides an appropriate map background overprinted with a route to the passenger's check-in point. This system has helped to overcome the often very stressful problem of navigating between one form of transport and another.

Vehicle drivers are on the whole well catered for in terms of the signing of major roads and motorways, which is now based on the requirements of realistic vehicle speeds, poor

centre of its rather bulky CRT screen. The map scale could zoom from the size of an entire city area down to individual streets.

With satellite-positioning systems today, the biggest challenge is probably the design problem involved in producing a clear, simple screen interface which does not distract drivers and which gives them a choice between different types of display, including verbal instructions and graphic symbols such as arrows and pictograms. Serious thought is being given to a version of the head-up display used in some fighter aircraft as being the safest and most user-friendly option.

An important aspect of signing is the planning of orientation systems designed for the interiors of buildings, particularly large and complex public buildings such as museums, hospitals and libraries (pp. 138–39 [1–3]). It is now quite common to provide computer 'kiosks' within the main entrances of buildings to enable visitors to locate the areas or rooms they wish to visit and to print out standard plans with overprinted routes to their destinations. The National Gallery in London has for several years used screen-based information in its 'Micro Gallery', which enables the visitor to select a list of paintings from a touch-screen and to print out a plan indicating their exact location within particular galleries. Similar information kiosks are now a common feature of internal signing systems and provide a much larger range of information than is possible with static signing. Besides allowing particular exhibits to be located, they can be used to alert visitors to items which are no longer on display.

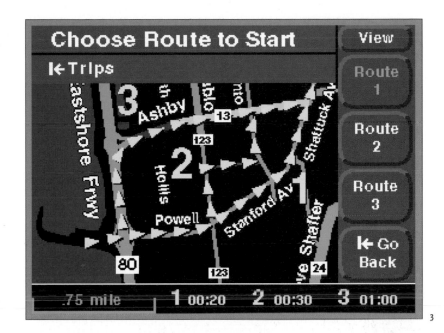

3

4

**Experimental Navigation Interfaces**

These two screens for a vehicle navigation system show selected routes at different scales with summaries in the bottom panel. The lower screen includes weather information. *Design: Aaron Marcus and Associates, Inc., U.S.A.; client: Motorola, Inc./Automotive and Industrial Electronics Group, U.S.A.*

Between 1991 and 1994, a new signing system was devised by the designers together with the Schiphol Airport design department. This is a comprehensive system incorporating typography and colour coding for road as well as interior signing, flight information displays and maps [1–2] and is being continually developed. The colour system is partly based on the original 1960s system created by Benno Wissing (Total Design); blue is used for roads, and yellow and green are used inside the terminal for operational facilities information. Grey is used for non-directional information and black for office areas, while red and green also appear, to designate (stop, danger) and (exit, confirmation) respectively. The Schiphol colour scheme has proven to be very successful mainly because of the high legibility and clarity of text, particularly from a distance.

1

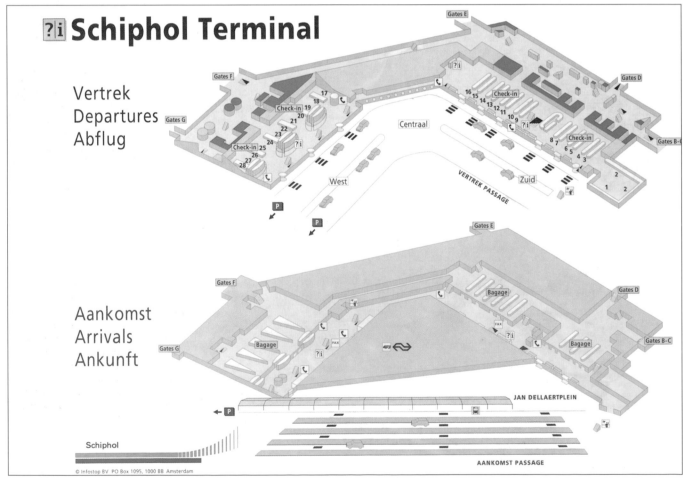

2

3

---

**Aankomst / Paspoortcontrole**
Arrivals / Immigration ↗

**Alle landen**
All countries **Balies** 1 **en** 2
Desks **and**

 **Alleen Europese Gemeenschap**
European Community only **Balies** 3 **en** 4
Desks **and**

4

---

←  **Uitgang**
Exit

 **Douane**
Customs

 **Bagagebanden 1 t/m 18**
Baggage belts 1 to 18

 **Bagageservice**
Baggage service

5

**3 – 5**
**Schiphol Airport Signing**

The type-face used is Frutiger with some modifications for use on CRT-displays (of which there are more than fifteen hundred) and internally illuminated signs. All the signs are bilingual (Dutch-English), with the Dutch in Frutiger Bold and the English in Frutiger Light (fractionally smaller to emphasize the contrast). The pictograms which supplement the text are based on the U.S. Department of Transportation (DOT) and isotype public information symbols series.
*Design: Bureau Mijksenaar and Design Department of Amsterdam Airport Schiphol, The Netherlands*

1

2

3

1 – 3
**Düsseldorf Airport Signing**

In April 1996, a disastrous fire broke out at Düsseldorf Airport which resulted in a number of fatalities. A spokesperson for the city's fire brigade blamed the large number of casualties on passengers who ignored emergency exit signing. Having had the signing singled out as a contributing factor in the disaster, the airport management were determined that proper signing would be a priority when the facility was rebuilt. Meta Design were selected to produce a temporary system to enable the airport to continue to operate during reconstruction and to form the basis for a permanent signing system.

5

4

4 – 5
**Düsseldorf Airport Signing**

Having analyzed approximately fifteen hundred existing signs in the airport, Meta Design determined that half of them were redundant. A structural hierarchy was developed for the new system, with information organized according to immediate importance. For instance, departure signs were shown before arrivals as it was felt that departing passengers would be in more of a hurry than arriving ones. Colour coding was used; transportation signs employed white type on green, while service information used white on grey. Particular attention was paid to the emergency signs; a striking yellow-green was selected for immediate visibility. All signs had to be legible from a distance of a hundred feet, so type-face was an important factor, especially in view of the airport's variety of lighting types. 'Info' was used because it takes up to twelve per cent less space than other faces such as Helvetica or Univers. The pictograms, designed for the Berlin Transit Authority, were based on the system used for the 1972 Munich Olympics. Interestingly, a year after completion the airport information desk noticed a fifty-per-cent drop in the number of inquiries.
*Design: MetaDesign, Germany, U.K. and U.S.A.*

**Marine Gate Signing System**

As part of a revitalization programme, the Japanese city of Shiogama, in Miyagi Prefecture, sought a combined signing and colour identity system. The design plan was originally applied in the old port terminal building, but the concept had to be flexible enough to be used in other parts of the city as they were developed. Thus, it had to be able to respond to a wide variety of architectural styles and yet retain a recognizable city identity, which it established by means of two fundamental elements: local form and colour.

1

海鮮市
Kaisen-ichi (Fresh Seafood Market)

↗
北ゲート
North Gate

2

Historically, the city of Shiogama has been associated with salt and its refinement; even today, there is a shrine dedicated to the god of salt there. Drawing on this theme, the designers based the grid for the signing and printed matter on the chemical lattice structure of the salt crystal. The second element, colour, was split into two components. The base colour was chosen to harmonize with the colour of local buildings and streets, and was therefore used primarily as a background colour. The second colour scheme relied on bold primary colours which recalled the harbour's nautical feeling. These tones were applied mainly to temporary banners [2] – like signal flags – and signs.

*Design: Masahiko Kimura, gk Graphics, Japan*

3

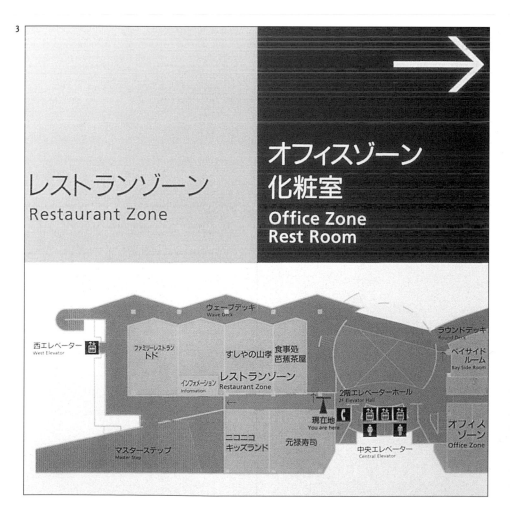

4

5

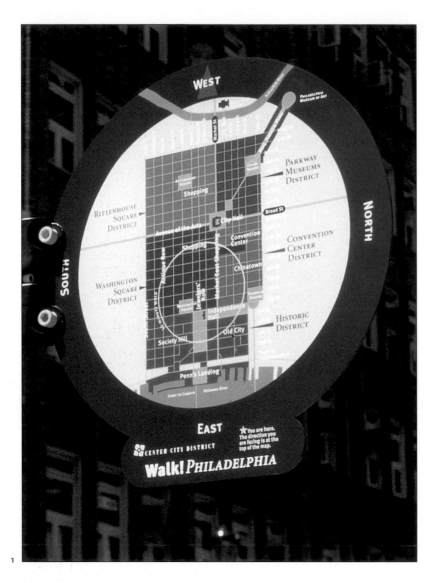

1

2

1 – 2

**Philadelphia City Centre Signing**

A comprehensive pedestrian street signing scheme which consists of more than a thousand directional and disc signs has been developed for the pedestrian area of Philadelphia, Pennsylvania, as part of a street-scape improvement project. The system includes new lighting, trees, paving and street furniture; the project has been funded by a tax on property owners and tenants in the area. The area was divided into five districts based loosely on William Penn's original plan for the city, with the major streets serving as boundaries. Icons were used on signs together with colour coding for each district, and each large disc sign [1] carries a circular map which equates to a ten-minute walk.
*Design: Joel Katz,*
*Katz Wheeler Design,*
*U.S.A.*

**3 – 4**
**Monte Veritá Signing**

Monte Veritá is an historic building run by a public foundation set up by the Canton, the Swiss Federal Institute of Technology and the Township of Ascona. The area, associated in the past with such notable figures as Sophie and Hans Arp, Oskar Schlemmer, Paul Klee, Erich Maria Remarque and Carl Jung, has a strong cultural tradition in the arts, sciences and politics.
*Design: Studio di Progettazione Grafica, Switzerland*

3

4

6

5

**5 – 6**
**Waterloo International Station Signing**

These directional signs in English and French for the Eurostar departure terminal at Waterloo International are part of a general signing system for which the client stipulated that the signs be kept clear of the roof surface, which was initially conceived as temporary.
*Design: Henrion, Ludlow & Schmidt, U.K.*

1

2

3

**1 – 3**
**Signing and Visual Identity for Cité Internationale de Lyon**

The Cité Internationale de Lyon, designed by Renzo Piano, is a new site which unites a museum of contemporary art, a congress centre, cinemas, hotels and offices. This territorial identity system is based on a background pattern of variable textile weft.

*Design: Ruedi Baur, Denis Coueinoux, Chantal Grossen and Felix Müller, Intégral: Ruedi Baur et Associés, France*

**4 – 5**
**Signing for the Domaine de Chambord**

The Domaine de Chambord is a huge forest surrounding Chambord castle in France. The signs are three-dimensional clay structures of varying sizes and cross-sections.

**6 – 7**
**Signing for the Domaine de Chambord**

Architectural elements in their own right, the L-shaped information posts evoke the castle by means of their colour and geometric form. *Design: Ruedi Baur, Eva Kubinyi and Ludovic Vallognes in collaboration with Laurent Lacour (pictograms) and Jacqueline Osty (landscaping), Intégral: Ruedi Baur et Associés, France*

1

**1 – 3**
**RAC Corporate Identity**

Thank you for visiting
Please drive carefully

RAC

2

Exit

RAC

3

Signage forms only one part of Britain's new Royal Automobile Club corporate identity, which was redesigned to signal the company's new image to customers, to the public, to its partners and to its competitors. The designers worked closely with a number of specialists: scientists, to develop the high-visibility orange paint for the vans; the police and colour experts, on the safety and visibility aspects of rescue vehicles; a clothing company, for high-performance uniforms; and architects and sculptors, for the signage's structure. The on-site signage [1–3] was a low-cost replacement for a previous sign system. An aluminium sleeve was devised that would slide over an existing shell.

The roadside signing follows strict u.k. transportation guidelines, which stipulate colour and type-face and consists of clear rectangular decals with white letterforms. The signage must be created quickly, sometimes on the spot, to aid motorists going to RAC-affiliated events. The signs have an exposed grid of equal increments so as to enable the end-user to establish hanglines and tabulation [4–5]. The corporate typography was applied using digitally cut vinyl lettering in keeping with the signage grid specifications [6] and the mandatory use of Jock Kinneir's Transport type-face. The designers commissioned typographers Dalton Maag to create the digital cut.

*Design: Simon Browning, Tim Beard, Sean Perkins, Paul Austin, Mason Wells, Ben Parker, Rupert Bassett and Sean Murphy, North Design, London; client: Royal Automobile Club, u.k.*

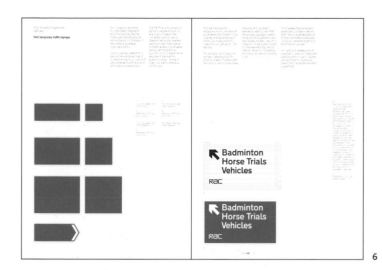

6

4

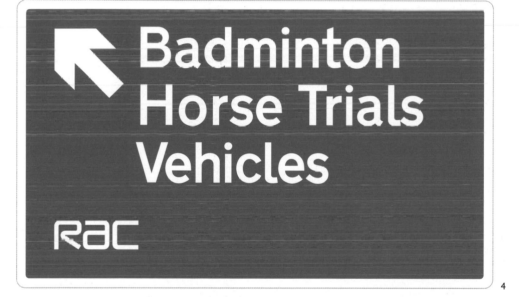

5

1

2

1 — 2

**Bundestag Building Identity**

The open plan and generous use of glass in the new Bundestag in Bonn made a special approach to communication essential. The concept proposed by the design office of Baumann and Baumann is much more than a signing system; it is both a corporate identity and a cultural communication model. The open plan required an approach which was both flexibly authoritative and politically neutral. The graphic elements consist of a symbol based on the Bundestag's seating layout; the type-face is Rotis, which is used for all signing and printed matter.

3

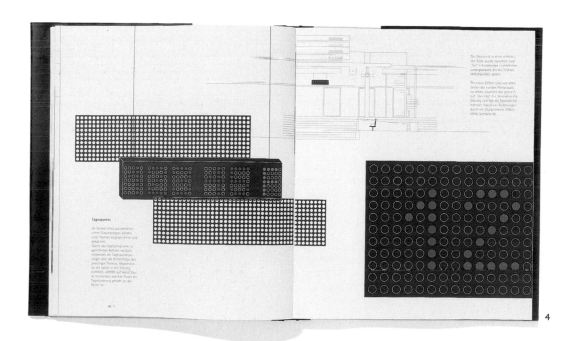

4

**3 – 4**
**Bundestag Building Identity**

All of these spreads are from
the book which documents
the four-year design process.
All aspects of the signing,
colour system and type-face –
even the clock face – were
specially designed. There is
also a section on the poetry
mural by the Austrian poet
Ernst Jandl, a detail of which
is used for the book's title,
*Lechts rinks*. Illustrated here
are the main external entrance
sign [1], the external signing
[2], the safety signs for the
lobby areas [3] and the
electronic displays [4].
*Design: Baumann and
Baumann, Schwäbisch Gmünd,
Germany; publisher: Hatje,
Germany*

This CD-ROM was created to combine the Automobile Association's atlas mapping routes and tourist information. It was partly developed in-house at the AA and partly by a third party in the United States. The interface was designed to be simple and user-friendly.The overall design concept had to retain the AA's cartographic style and follow established corporate guidelines for graphics, including the 'house' colours, yellow and black, although these were intensified to work better on screen. One important feature of the CD is the possibility of printing out a section for a specific journey.
*Design: Automobile Association, U.K.*

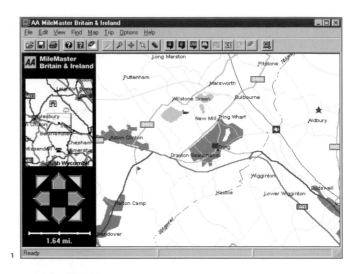

1

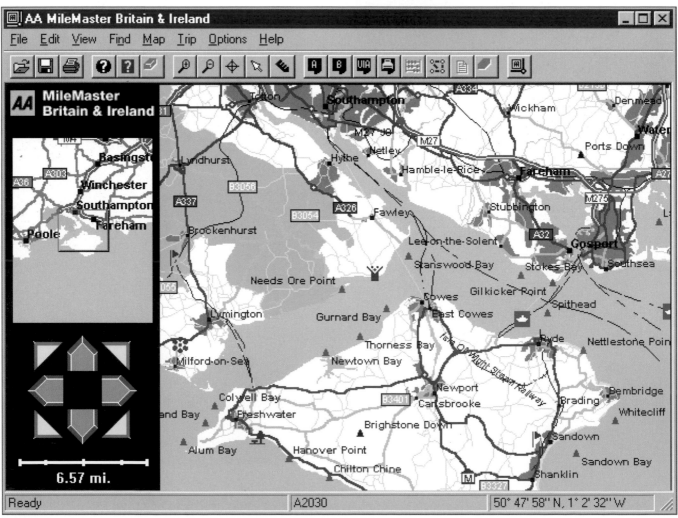

2

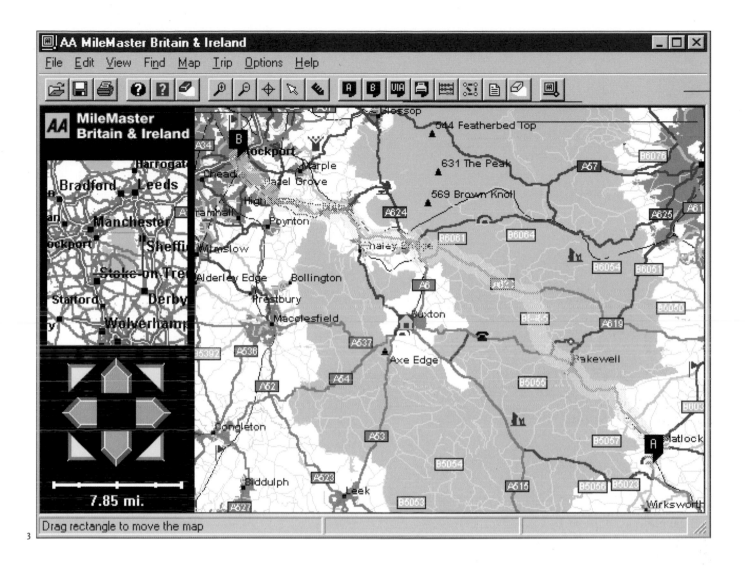

# Electronic In-Car Navigation Aid
## Designing the Screen Display

Routefinder was a small electronic navigation device for drivers, fitted with a data card containing the Automobile Association's database of 38,000 places in mainland Britain, and the routes between them – a poor man's version of the more sophisticated but very expensive Global Positioning Satellite (GPS)-based systems.

The product, originally an *Innovations*-type gadget, had been taken on by Philips Car Systems, to be repackaged, developed and marketed as a mainstream car accessory. The original software team invented the device, creating a routing algorithm together with a way of compressing a vast amount of data on a small removable chip.

Our initial brief was to design a set of symbols for road junctions, road types and landmarks. The symbols had to be instantly recognizable and self-explanatory to a driver on the road without the time or opportunity to refer to any explanation. It quickly became apparent that the screen information would not be legible enough in normal driving conditions; the software developers had created an emboldened character set, believing that this would be more visible – in practice, it diminished clarity, and the characters were too bulky to permit many characters per line. A larger screen/higher resolution/backlighting (the ideal solution) were too expensive; the alternative was to design a more legible alphabet and an integrated set of symbols with the aim of saving space and aiding rapid reading. Two alphabet and symbol sets were developed, one for set-up and gazetteer (twelve pixels high) and one for routing (fifteen pixels high), and a set of key legends. Working with reference to research papers from the Department of Transport, and assuming an eye-to-screen distance of about 700 mm to the dashboard-mounted device, it became clear that even this would not be enough to help a driver to read the information within the maximum safe glance time of less than two seconds. The database, though full of informative detail, was text-based, unstructured and difficult to display on such a small screen. We analyzed the information and found it to be reasonably well organized for its original use but badly structured for its new use. Time and cost factors precluded fundamental changes, but the worst excesses were tidied, making the text less discursive and more concise. A project which started with the design of a few symbols grew to include alphabet design, screen layout, software mapping, information

1

The driver plans a route in advance on the hand-held device, which is then slotted into a dashboard-mounted unit. The route is played back during the journey.

```
┌─────────────────────────────────┐
│   Westminster Bridge - Dover     │
│  ─────────────────────────────   │
│  Distance: 76.9 miles            │
│  Time: 1 hour 41 minutes         │
│  Cost: £5.69                     │
│  Fuel: 9.70 litres               │
│  ETA: 12.24                      │
│  ╭──────┬───────┬──────╮         │
│  │ ESC  │ PRINT │  OK  │         │
│  ╰──────┴───────┴──────╯         │
└─────────────────────────────────┘
```

2

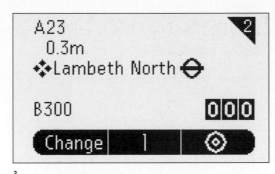

```
┌─────────────────────────────────┐
│  A23                         ◤2  │
│   0.3m                           │
│  ❖ Lambeth North         ⊖       │
│                                  │
│  B300                   [0][0][0]│
│  ╭──────────┬───────┬──────╮     │
│  │ Change   │   1   │  ◎   │     │
│  ╰──────────┴───────┴──────╯     │
└─────────────────────────────────┘
```

3

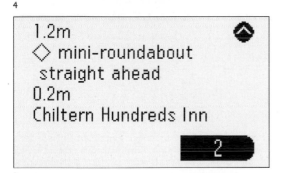

```
┌─────────────────────────────────┐
│  A20                         ◤1  │
│   12.7m                          │
│  ❖ M20 M25                       │
│                                  │
│  M20                    [0][1][7]│
│  ╭──────────┬───────────╮        │
│  │ Change   │     2     │        │
│  ╰──────────┴───────────╯        │
└─────────────────────────────────┘
```

4

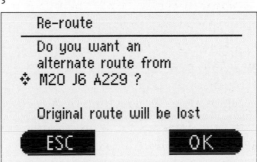

```
┌─────────────────────────────────┐
│   Re-route                       │
│  ─────────────────────────────   │
│  Do you want an                  │
│  alternate route from            │
│  ❖ M20 J6 A229 ?                 │
│                                  │
│  Original route will be lost     │
│  ╭──────────╮       ╭──────────╮ │
│  │   ESC    │       │    OK    │ │
│  ╰──────────╯       ╰──────────╯ │
└─────────────────────────────────┘
```

5

```
┌─────────────────────────────────┐
│  1.2m                        ⬆   │
│  ◇ mini-roundabout               │
│    straight ahead                │
│  0.2m                            │
│  Chiltern Hundreds Inn           │
│                    ╭──────────╮  │
│                    │    2     │  │
│                    ╰──────────╯  │
└─────────────────────────────────┘
```

6

```
┌─────────────────────────────────┐
│  ❖ A2                            │
│  ◇ roundabout                    │
│   1st main exit                  │
│  0.2m                            │
│  Dover Eastern Docks  ⛴          │
│                    ╭──────────╮  │
│                    │    2     │  │
│                    ╰──────────╯  │
└─────────────────────────────────┘
```

7

The Routefinder is designed to be easier and safer to use while driving than a road map, with greater detail and functionality. Before the journey, the device calculates the time and cost for the planned trip (here, between Westminster Bridge, London, and the port of Dover) [2]. The journey starts and the screen shows the distance to the first landmark [3]. After seventeen miles, the screen displays which road the driver should be on [4]. At a certain point, the driver decides to take a detour [5], which prompts a more detailed screen giving alternative distances and landmarks [6]. Once on the detour, the driver is given instructions on how to return to the original route [7].

restructuring and user-manual design. Ideally, a product such as this should be operable without a manual, but with an innovative concept to be introduced and a product hurried to market with small problems remaining in the underlying software, it was necessary to explain and excuse some features which did not operate in the way that most users would naturally expect.

There was nothing remarkable about this work in pure design terms; we were applying well-worn principles and concepts. What was interesting was that information designers became part of the team at such a late stage. The product is a brilliant idea. It had excellent potential. But the project suffered at the planning stage from a lack of understanding of the ergonomics of displays and the need to analyze and structure information. It remains a good illustration of the interrelationships in information design – between product, user, design, software, manufacture, information provision – and the importance of being aware of them and managing them effectively.

*Gill Scott*

1

**1 – 4**
**Swiss National Railways Scenic Route Indicator**

Swiss National Railways run a special panoramic train serving one of the most important scenic routes in Switzerland, which takes in Luzern, Brünnig and Interlaken. In 1996, the Basel design office of Hoffmann-Stahli was commissioned to produce a graphic device as a tourist guide for use in the trains. After a series of black and white roughs were made, an example of which is shown [2], the Scenic Route Indicator [frontis., 3–4] was designed to interpret the landscape and indicate its major distinguishing features. The route diagram represents the characteristics of the landscape as viewed by the passengers; unlike a conventional map, the Indicator shows the traveller's orientation to the landscape. The four Swiss lakes are presented accurately depending on the direction of travel. The Indicator is located next to the carriage window [1] rather like a table and remains viable even though the train changes direction due to a cul-de-sac along the route.
*Design: Sandra Hoffmann, Hoffmann-Stahli Basel, Switzerland*

2

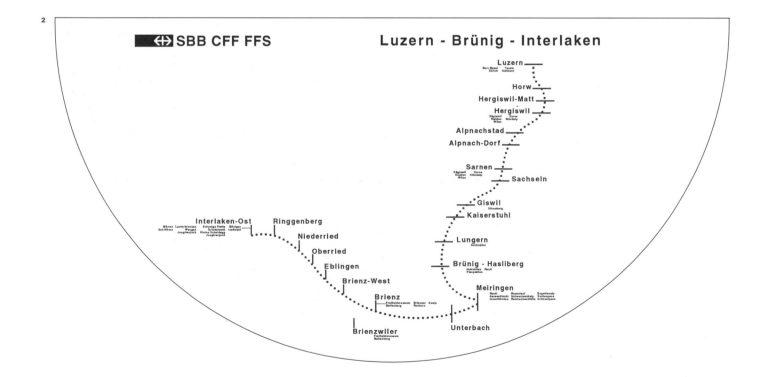

3

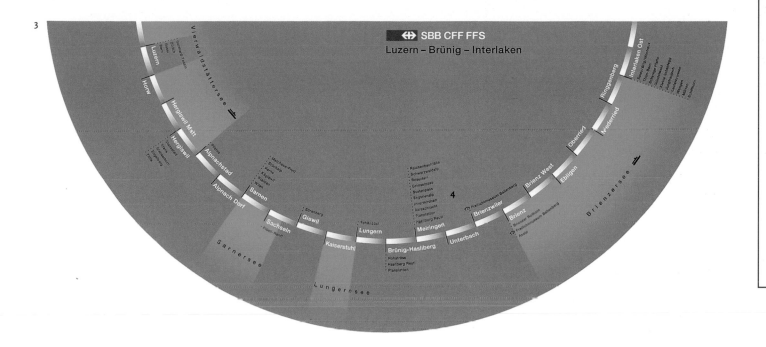

SBB CFF FFS
Luzern – Brünig – Interlaken

4

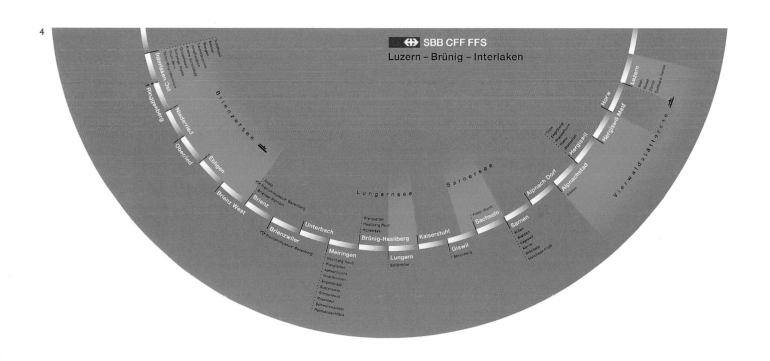

SBB CFF FFS
Luzern – Brünig – Interlaken

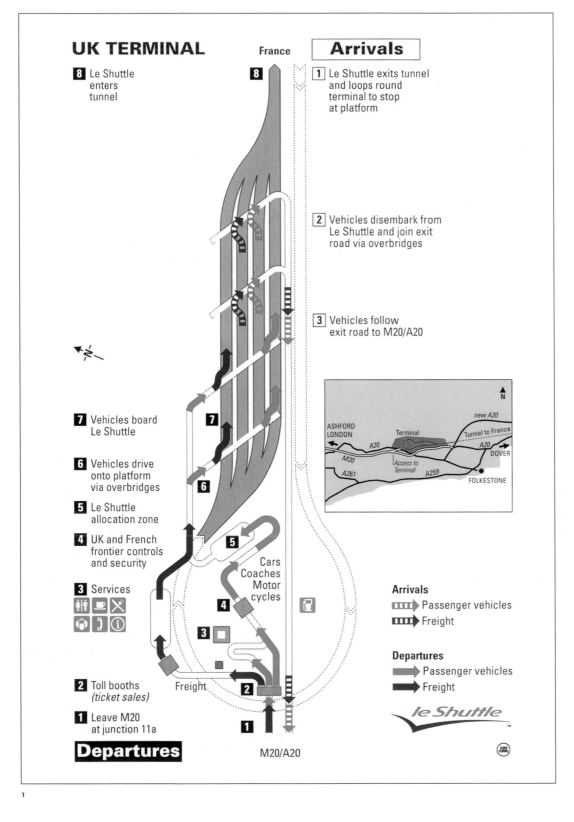

**UK TERMINAL**    France    **Arrivals**

**8** Le Shuttle enters tunnel

**8**

**1** Le Shuttle exits tunnel and loops round terminal to stop at platform

**2** Vehicles disembark from Le Shuttle and join exit road via overbridges

**3** Vehicles follow exit road to M20/A20

**7** Vehicles board Le Shuttle

**6** Vehicles drive onto platform via overbridges

**5** Le Shuttle allocation zone

**4** UK and French frontier controls and security

**3** Services

**2** Toll booths *(ticket sales)*

**1** Leave M20 at junction 11a

**Departures**

Cars Coaches Motor cycles

Freight

**Arrivals**

▦▶ Passenger vehicles
▦▶ Freight

**Departures**

➤ Passenger vehicles
➤ Freight

*le Shuttle* ™

M20/A20

Map inset:
ASHFORD LONDON — A20 — Terminal — new A20 — Tunnel to France — A20 — DOVER
M20 — Access to Terminal — A259 — FOLKESTONE
A261
N

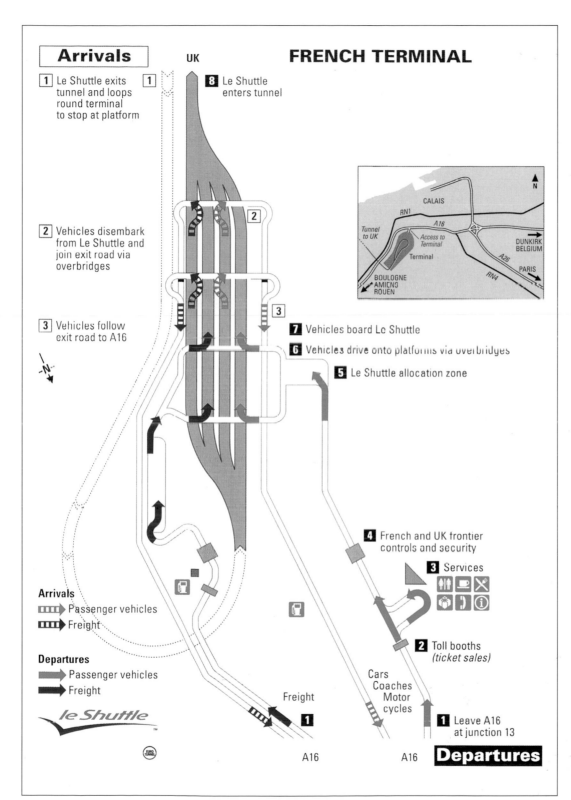

**Arrivals**

**1** Le Shuttle exits tunnel and loops round terminal to stop at platform

**2** Vehicles disembark from Le Shuttle and join exit road via overbridges

**3** Vehicles follow exit road to A16

**FRENCH TERMINAL**

UK

**8** Le Shuttle enters tunnel

CALAIS
RN1
A16
Tunnel to UK
Access to Terminal
Terminal
DUNKIRK BELGIUM
A26
PARIS
RN4
BOULOGNE
AMIENS
ROUEN
N

**7** Vehicles board Le Shuttle

**6** Vehicles drive onto platforms via overbridges

**5** Le Shuttle allocation zone

**4** French and UK frontier controls and security

**3** Services

**2** Toll booths (ticket sales)

Cars Coaches Motor cycles

**1** Leave A16 at junction 13

**Arrivals**
Passenger vehicles
Freight

**Departures**
Passenger vehicles
Freight

le Shuttle

Freight

**1**

A16

A16

**Departures**

2

**1 – 2
Eurotunnel Maps**

These two maps illustrate the terminal layouts at Dover and Calais, at either end of the Channel Tunnel. The objective was to emphasize the simplicity of moving through the embarkation/disembarkation process. There are two versions of the maps, one for freight and one for passengers. As the terminals were still under construction when the maps were initiated, the layouts had to be distilled from engineering site plans. Drawn on a computer, they were devised to work both in black and white and in colour and in any language (of which there initially were four). *Design: Trevor Bounford, Chapman Bounford and Associates, U.K.*

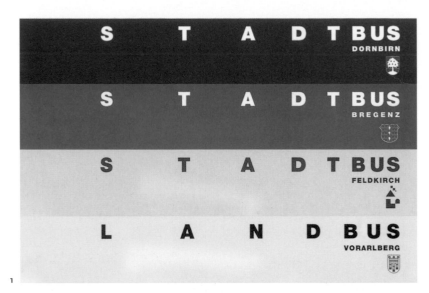

1

**Vorarlberg Public Transport System**

In the last few years, Vorarlberg, the western province of Austria, has witnessed the development of an exemplary integrated public transport network. It includes four city bus routes (Vorarlberg, Feldkirch, Bregenz, Dornbirn) and a country bus route, identified graphically as *Stadtbus* or *Landbus* [1]. It is to the credit of the Vorarlberg regional authority that they had the foresight to commission the Luger design studio to carry out this comprehensive corporate concept and signing system, which was planned down to the smallest detail, from timetables to compatible street furniture.

2

3

4

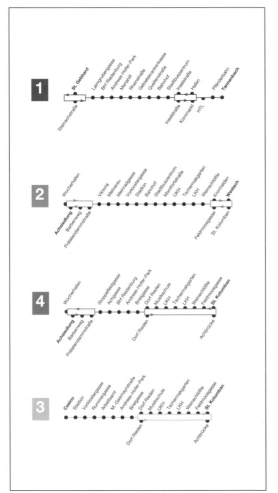

5

6

## 7 – 8
## Vorarlberg Public Transport System

Colour coding was used to distinguish the different bus routes, including relevant printed materials such as timetables, network maps and tickets but also bus stops and ticket machines.
The external livery of the buses is complemented by the interior colour co-ordination.
*Design: Reinhold Luger, Austria*

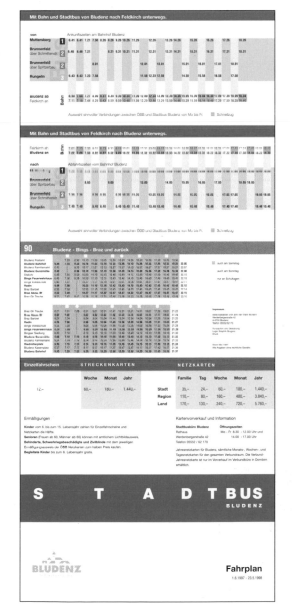

7

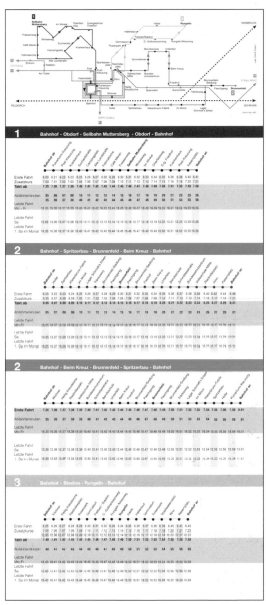

8

1

2

**1 – 2**
**Buenos Aires Underground System**

In the past few years, one Argentinean design office has undertaken some very large projects, particularly in the public sector. The latest and perhaps the most complex is the signing for the Buenos Aires underground system. The project began with the re-designing of Callaldo and Tribuales stations as prototypes, closely followed by Retiro station. Colour coding was used to designate the metro lines [**1**, **5**]; the Frutiger type-face family was used throughout. Various sign types were employed, including flag and suspended signs [**2**, **4**] and the main type, a longitudinal or strip sign referred to in the project as the main strip [**3**].

3

4

The main strips [3] carry
the main station information
and are divided into two
horizontal zones. The top
section repeats the name
of the station at regular
intervals, while the lower
section lists exits, street-
level landmarks and
directional arrows.
*Design: Estudio Shakespear,
Argentina*

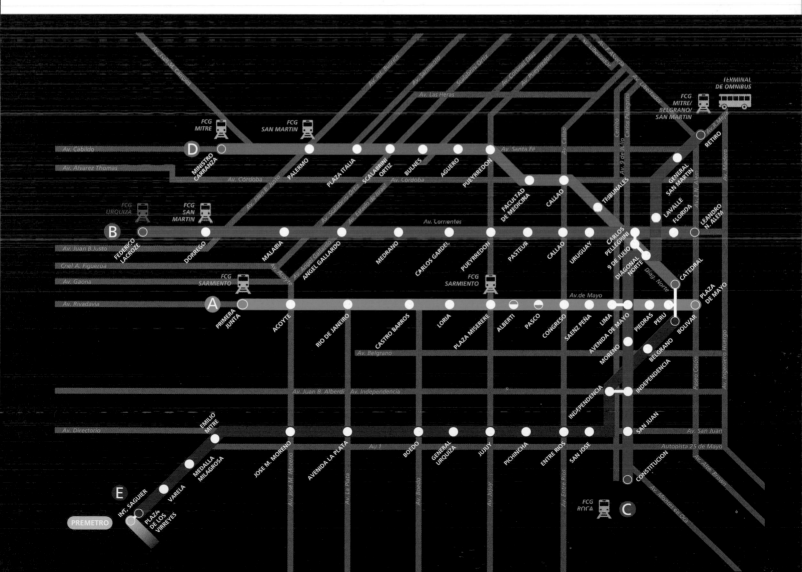

1 – 3
**Berlin Transportation Signing**

The principal problem facing the designer was, as with the infrastructure of Berlin itself, to unify two systems which had been cut off from each other while integrating a redesigned system which accommodated the expanded and expanding transportation network, including bus, underground and commuter train services. A symptom of the problem is apparent in a sign in the former East Berlin underground [3].

2

3

1

The uniformity of typographic treatment across all the transportation systems is evident in the new underground signage [1], which relates closely to the wall-mounted strip map [2] showing an underground line. At first sight, the redesigned rail-system map – comprising underground and commuter services – appears to be similar to London's classic example. Closer scrutiny, however, reveals that the Berlin system contains several networks and great detail, while adhering to the devices established for each individual network.

*Design: MetaDesign, Berlin*

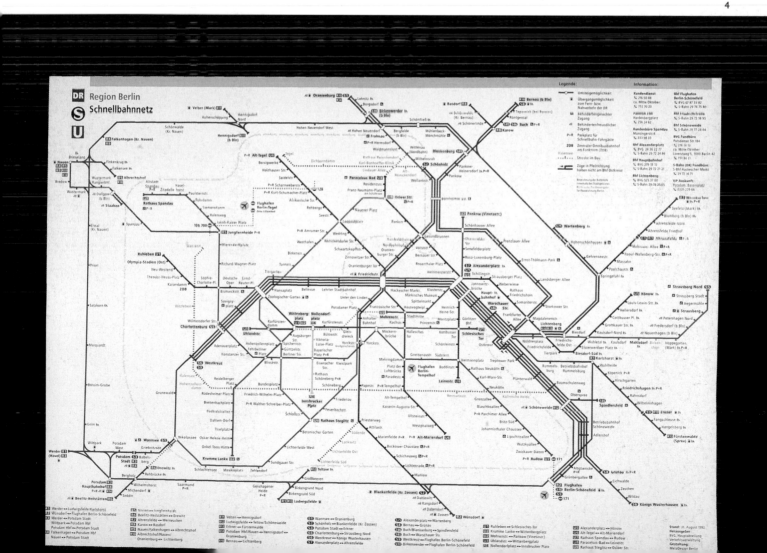

# Schwäbisch Gmünd Bus Station
## Integrating a New Signing System

A major component of the concept was the design of the timetables for the complete network.

Schwäbisch Gmünd, a mainly medieval town in southern Germany, presented several interesting problems to the designers who were asked to provide efficient and visually satisfying signage for its bus system. The signage had to be planned in such a way that it would be sympathetic to the existing building style and fit in with an established town signing system. What made the project almost unique was that the concept of an important transportation hub was rethought by the town's administration, and the funds were found for a completely new station complex in which the graphic elements of bus identification, extensive signing, maps, route plans and timetables were closely integrated.

The scheme had to give the town not only a transportation system which would provide an attractive alternative to the car but also a strong focal point within its infrastructure for the many privately run buses. The existing bus station was a very unattractive building surrounded by a vast area of concrete and tarmac which did nothing to promote bus travel. Right from the planning stage, the town administrators decided to commission a new station building and a completely new environment for the surrounding area, to provide a welcome for arriving passengers as well as information about destinations and routes. It was also decided that the new bus station should provide pleasant surroundings for passengers

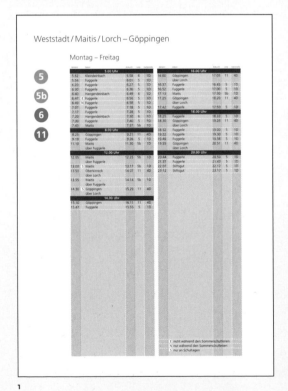

1

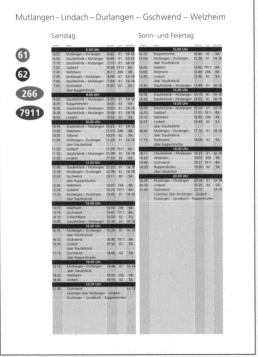

2

3      4      5      6

7

awaiting connections. To make the whole area less like an enormous car park, a new setting was planned with covered parking bays, sheltered waiting and boarding points and generous seating arrangements.

The new bus station building, designed by Professor Peter Schenk and architect Thomas Weinig, is mainly of glass and steel construction, giving it a light, transparent and functional appearance. An integral part of the design of the interior was the provision of information areas for the display of large route maps for both local and regional buses as well as timetables and other information.

As with airport buildings, there is a clear separation of the plan into two distinct zones: the waiting and information area, and the arrival and departure points. The waiting area is circular in plan and strongly cylindrical in elevation, giving it a cohesive form and acting as a strong visual

landmark when seen at a distance. Within this waiting area, passengers have access to the usual facilities, information on the complete bus system and a town map. Since the new station is served daily by about six hundred buses and is used by several thousand regular commuters, this makes for a complex information system.

The key document in drawing all of this information together is the route map, which, in its redesigned form, manages to link these services into a coherent whole. The sheer amount of information ruled out a conventional town plan type of map and was structured instead as a network map using a geometrical grid split into two distinct sections (the difference in scales precluded the use of a single map).

The signing system is used sparingly throughout, and each sign is carefully positioned only where the traveller has to make a decision. The signs themselves are based on a six-by-six-inch

3 – 7

Illustrated here are the narrow-format signs which are based on the six-by-six-inch module. One can see clearly the very graphic treatment of the individual signs which indicate the immediate facilities in and around the central bus station.

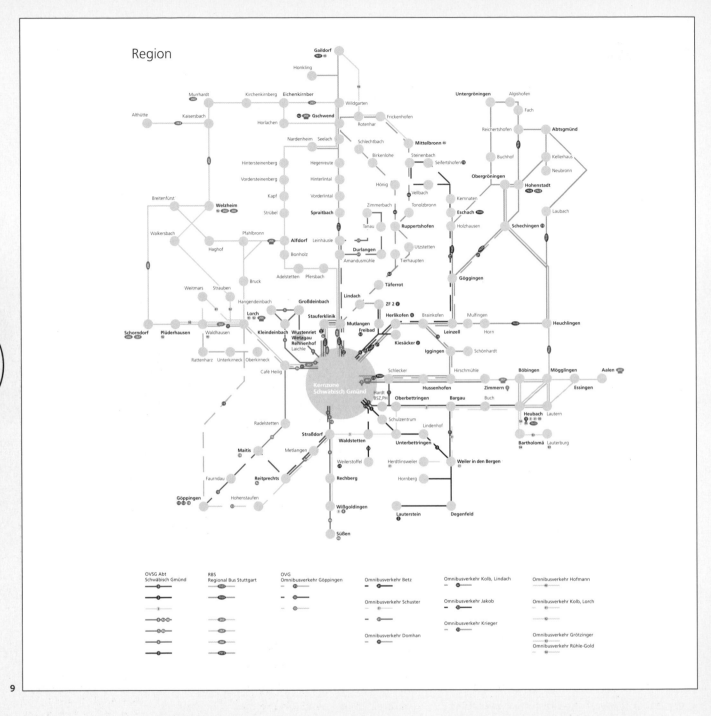

Region

module and are constructed of narrow-section steel and aluminium which has been sprayed or lacquered and positioned between stainless steel uprights. These uprights provide minimum obstruction but are of sufficient strength and longevity to fulfil their function. Most of the signs make use of glass rather than transparent plastic, and this has proven to be

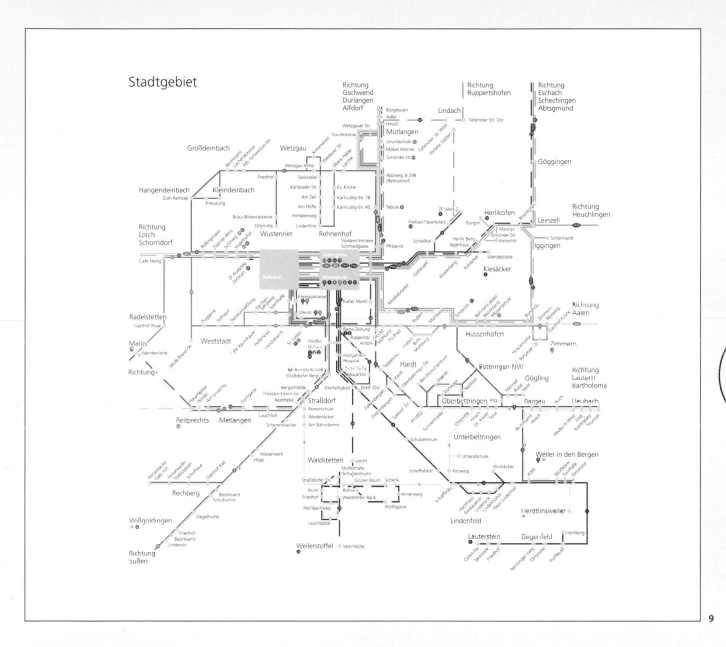

Stadtgebiet

Case Study

9

highly resistant to vandalism and, to date, has not had to be replaced.

Type which has to be legible from a distance requires slightly different characteristics from type used at normal reading distance and read as continuous text. The type-face used for the bus signing scheme and for the general town signing is Frutiger. This sans serif type-face is characterized by having a well-detailed alphabet and an open form which lends itself to legibility at a distance.

Of the other visual elements, colour plays an important role in distinguishing the various bus companies in conjunction with a bold numbering system. Colours used in the signing were limited to a maximum of five so as to avoid confusion in such a small area.                    *Ulrich Schwarz*

8 – 9

These bus-route maps illustrate the use of colour and type. [8] is the regional map, while [9] shows the area of the town.

# 2 Explaining How Things Work

**Flow Diagrams • Photomontages • Statistical Diagrams • Newspaper Graphics • Medical Diagrams Structures and Actions • Installation Instructions • Manufacturing Processes**

The earliest form of printed information in graphic form is probably to be found in the encyclopaedias of Denis Diderot, first published in 1751. Of the seventeen volumes, eleven were illustrated with copper-plate engravings which provide a mirror of eighteenth-century life, depicting every aspect of the culture, manufacturing and craft of the period. These volumes anticipated the development of the explanatory treatise that occurred over the next 250 years. The invention of half-tone and especially multicolour printing in the nineteenth century enabled artists to depict information of all kinds in a much more attractive and popular form, although the early half-tones were not capable of the precise definition of the copper-plate engraving. One area in which colour was put to good effect in the 1800s was the presentation of anatomical illustrations using a series of layered flaps to show the complexity of the human body convincingly.

The 1900s saw the rise of ever more complex manufactured products and processes which challenged the conventional methods of representation and led to the invention of new graphic techniques to explain a product to its user. These ranged from cut-away and cross-sectional diagrams to the 'exploded' view which could represent every component making up a product as well as its sequence of assembly. Exploded views had the added benefit of allowing the identification of every part of a product by name or number, thus simplifying the ordering of spare parts in the age of mass production and anticipating the computerized ordering systems developed in the last decade.

During the 1930s – a great period for children's books in general – boys were especially well catered for by the Christmas annuals as well as by the weekly comic papers, some of which featured highly

**LONDON'S STREAMLINED TUBE TRAIN**

There are four of these trains made up of six cars each and developing 1,616 h.p., running on 600 volts D.C. They have greater acceleration and braking power and are now in service on the Piccadilly Line.

A great feature is that all the control gear and motors, etc., are beneath the floor, thus giving greater seating capacity. The rail clearance to do this is only sixteen inches.

1. Section through London clay
2. Concrete lining   3. Section of steel tunnel
4. Asbestos-lined tunnel to eliminate noise
5. 5A. Electric windscreen wipers
6. Driver's loud-speaker
7. Tunnel lighting unit for workmen
8. Tunnel lighting cable   9. Telephone cables
10. Automatic signal cables   11. Power cable
12. Hand-rail   13. Brake gauges
14. Electro-pneumatic brake handle
15. Automatic air brake handle
16. Inertia control   17. Automatic coupling
18. 18A. Live rails   19. Insulator
20. Concrete foundation for track
21. Face-plate controller
22. 22A. Contact shoes   23. Air reservoir
24. Power bogie   25. Brake cylinder and shoe
26. 110 h.p. traction motor   27. Driving gears
28. Extra space for passengers instead of the old motor-room

**Drawing by L. Ashwell Wood**

L. Ashwell Wood's cut-away drawing of 'London's Streamlined Tube Train' was used as a cover illustration to *Modern Wonder* (1938), a weekly boys' magazine of the period. Wood is probably best known for the double-page spreads which regularly appeared as the centrefold of *Eagle* magazine and which featured drawings of new engineering marvels.

coloured cut-away drawings of current engineering wonders. One of the contributors to this book has declared that the romantic drawings by L. Ashwell Wood which regularly appeared in the *Eagle*'s centre spread 'fired his imagination, and he knew what he wanted to be when he grew up – not an engine driver but an engine drawer'. Ashwell Wood was a prolific illustrator, and his cut-aways included Donald Campbell's jet-engined 'Bluebird' car, the Vickers VC10 airliner and the hovercraft. He seems to have had a particular affinity for trains of all types, including those of the London Underground [1].

The 1960s and '70s were the age of DIY, and publishers responded with numerous guides and manuals on maintenance and repairs. The Reader's Digest Association were notable for their range of guides, which were easily recognized by their two-colour storyboard treatments. These deceptively simple instruction manuals combined the attractiveness and accessibility of the comic-strip convention with a rigorous picture grid of 40 x 44-mm image units and unvarying three-line captions. Where other guides employed full-colour imagery, the Reader's Digest guides were enlivened by a palette of about five or six mechanical tints. They were produced by various teams of designers (as indeed were many of the comic strips), but because of their rigidly imposed style maintained a remarkably consistant quality.

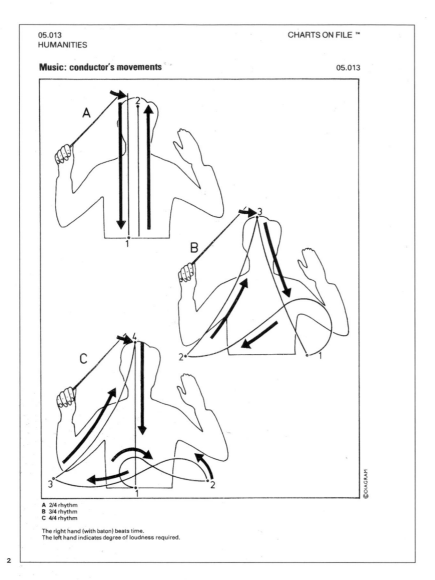

**Music: conductor's movements**      05.013

A   2/4 rhythm
B   3/4 rhythm
C   4/4 rhythm

The right hand (with baton) beats time.
The left hand indicates degree of loudness required.

2

### Conductor's Arm Movements

The complete volume of loose-leaf charts published as *Charts on File* consists of line charts with minimal captioning. They are arranged in sections ranging from 'Earth and Life Sciences' to 'Humanities' (from which this illustration is taken). *Concept: Diagram Visual Information Ltd, U.K.; publisher: Charts on File Inc., U.S.A.*

A book which established a new style benchmark was Diagram's *The Rules of the Game* of 1974, which inspired a whole series of illustrated action books. This book was organized in a completely different way from the Reader's Digest guides. Each double-page spread was devoted to one sport discipline and illustrated with a series of stylized action drawings. These were free of retaining frames and were set amidst a regular five-column typographical grid. Colour was used in two ways: as flat tints to define the parameters of the playing area or pitch, and as a series of pale tints to enliven the players' clothing. The book managed to compress large amounts of technical information about the rules of a given game together with numerous action sequences without ever appearing to be overcrowded, perhaps because the visual structure was always carefully controlled.

Other publishers of note of informational books in the 1980s were Future Books, Nordbok, Mitchell Beazley and the inexhaustible Dorling Kindersley, who have proven that accurate and skilful presentation of informational subjects (pp. 144–45 [1]) can be immensely popular both in printed and CD-ROM formats. Diagram also pioneered a new kind of informational book, the loose-leaf *Charts on File* of 1988, which included hundreds of diagrammatic sheets of black-and-white line images expressly intended to be copied for educational purposes [2].

One of the most influential scientific volumes of the 1980s was Philip and Phyllis Morrison's and Charles and Ray Eames's *Powers of Ten*, a book about the relative size of things in the universe and the effect of adding another zero (to quote its subtitle). Based on a film of the same name, this is a difficult book to classify [3–7]. It could be argued that it is the definitive 'version' since the film relies on simple animation of the key images to merge one with another, whereas the book amplifies each main image with other illustrations at a comparable scale. The concept is developed as a series of same-size square images of striking originality, with each image increasing or decreasing in scale by a factor of ten. Each of these images occupies a right-hand page whilst the facing page contains complementary illustrations at a comparable scale. This was probably the first time that mathematical descriptions of the universe had been translated into a purely visual system of communication and

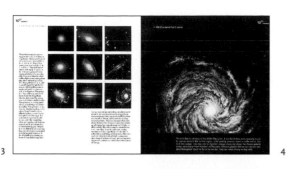

3

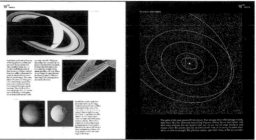

4

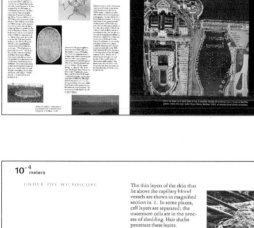

5

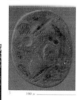

6

## Powers of Ten

The full title of this 1982 book, *Powers of Ten, a book about the relative size of things in the universe and the effect of adding another zero,* describes not only its subject but also the way the book is structured. The visual concept is of two squares, the larger of which contains an image and the smaller of which (in outline only) is centred on that image.
*Designers: Phillip and Phyllis Morrison and the Office of Charles and Ray Eames,* U.S.A.; *publisher: Scientific American Library,* U.S.A., *1982*

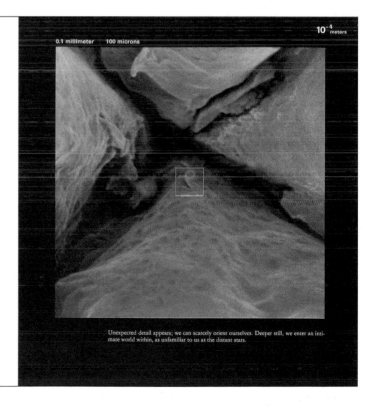

$10^{-4}$ meters

UNDER THE MICROSCOPE

The thin layers of the skin that lie above the capillary blood vessels are shown in magnified section in *1*. In some places, cell layers are separated; the outermost cells are in the process of shedding. Hair shafts penetrate these layers.

In *2* is a well known artifact of delicate detail, one we know better by ear than by eye: the grooves of a long-playing record. The very small portion seen takes only a couple of milliseconds to play. The wavy form of some grooves shows the scale of the recorded sound. The frequency range is a few thousands of reversals per second.

Another living freshwater ciliated protozoan is shown in *5*, replete with newly ingested strings of blue-green beads. These are filaments of widely found photosynthesizing bacteria.

Radiolaria are gorgeous minute marine creatures kin to the amoeba and important members of the zooplankton, especially in tropical seas. These pieces of exquisite lacework are the tests, or skeletal frameworks, of some forms. Unlike calcium-based bone and shell, these are made of translucent silica. The sea bottom contains such jewels as a major constituent over large areas. The photo *4* shows an example taken recently from the bottom ooze near the Azores; the drawing *3* is chosen from the compendium published by the scientist, artist, and philosopher Ernst Haeckel as part of the report of the renowned expedition of HMS *Challenger,* which sounded the ocean depths a century ago.

$10^{-4}$ meters

0.1 millimeter    100 microns

Unexpected detail appears; we can scarcely orient ourselves. Deeper still, we enter an intimate world within, as unfamiliar to us as the distant stars.

7

ISOTYPE **Diagram**

This typical isotype diagram compares home and factory weaving in England between 1820 and 1880, during the rise of the Industrial Revolution. Each blue symbol represents fifty million pounds of total production, each black figure ten thousand home weavers, and each orange figure ten thousand factory weavers.

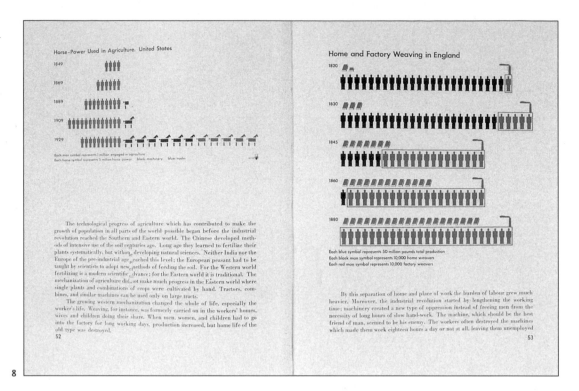

8

must rank with the achievements of William Playfair in reducing scientific data to a comprehensible whole. *Powers of Ten* was produced in the pre-computer era, so many of the images at both ends of the scale spectrum were created as artwork since the technology for recording them had not yet been invented. Another important science book published in the '80s was the outstanding pop-up volume by Jonathan Miller and David Pelham, *The Human Body*. This book went a stage beyond the nineteenth-century layered anatomical books mentioned earlier and showed the human body in three dimensions.

Another relevant category of information design from the same years consists of the mainly anonymous explanatory materials which accompanied almost every manufactured product from the simplest to the most complex. Much of this material had little to recommend it; many 'information' sheets from overseas manufacturers included frankly laughable translations of instructions and diagrams which often did not relate to the model in question. It seems likely that few of these instruction sheets and manuals were tested on the public before release.

In recent years, most of these problems have been solved. Attempts have been made to avoid the problem of having to translate texts into a number of languages by using pictograms instead of words. Success has depended on a close analysis of the story to be told, since pictograms have severe limitations in certain areas. They are best avoided if the result is likely to be ambiguous. For example, the concept of water is difficult to define graphically and the concept of drinking water even more difficult without resorting to words; any ambiguity can have dangerous health implications.

In certain contexts, a computer screen can provide the ideal form of instructional manual.

A machine can contain its own operating, maintenance, repair and help instructions, and a telephone hot-line can provide back-up if the manual proves to be inadequate. Alternative languages, instead of taking up the majority of the space as in a printed manual, can simply be substituted at will, whilst updates can be made as frequently as is necessary. Print-outs can be supplied for assimilation away from the machine or stored as a quickly accessible record. The variety of graphic techniques is almost unlimited, and besides colour and sound, both powerful elements in their own right, there is the added dimension of animation and the moving image.

As always, there are limitations, not the least of which is the cost factor, particularly for the memory necessary to store and read video. Also, few industrial or domestic products have a large enough screen to provide the definition required. Most hand-held products come with small non-illuminated screens capable of displaying just a few lines of text and rather primitive graphics. Nonetheless, in the area of maintenance, especially in the case of international businesses, the creation of on-screen manuals is being taken seriously (see pp. 70–73), especially since they can compete in cost with the considerable production and distribution expense of conventional printed documentation. The added benefits of rapid updating and an unlimited database are also attractive. A combination of static monitors and compact laptops could overcome previous flexibility problems in maintenance situations.

It is debatable whether money spent on well-designed and tested instruction manuals makes better sense than that spent on expensive technology. What is not in doubt is that manuals of the future will require designers experienced in the multi-disciplinary skills of multimedia production.

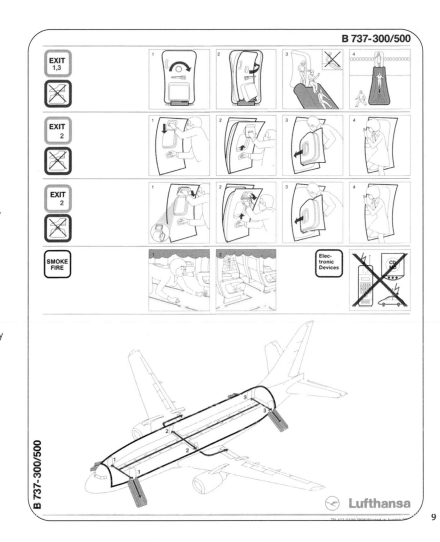

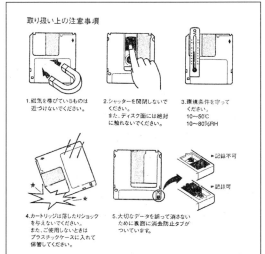

**Instruction Sheets**

The reverse of the Lufthansa safety chart [9] illustrated on page 16. The information leaflet about the handling of computer diskettes [10] uses both graphic and verbal techniques.

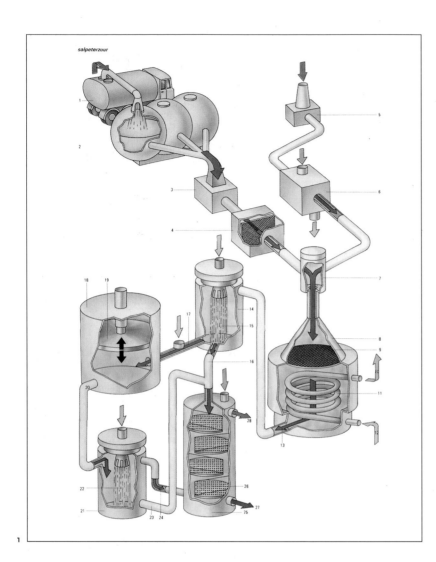

salpeterzuur

1

## Making Saltpetre

During the late 1970s, a twenty-four-part scientific encyclopaedia series was developed by Spectrum, a Dutch publisher. The diagram shown here describes the 'Ostwald' process for producing saltpetre for synthetic fertilizer. It illustrates well the fact that with logical routing, perspective and multi-layering, complicated and lengthy processes can be explained with a minimum of text and space.
*Design: Wim Crouwel, Total Design, The Netherlands; illustration: from* The Joy of Knowledge, *courtesy Mitchell Beazley, U.K.*

**2**

## Kansai International Airport

This is a cross-section of the new Kansai International Airport near Osaka in Japan. Kansai's closest rival airport, Narita near Tokyo, serves only international flights, while Kansai serves both international and inland flights. Many passengers use it as a transfer point, often spending more than two hours in the airport. The purpose of this diagram is to show the facilities such as shops and restaurants in the new airport building.
*Design: Hiroyuki Kimura, Tube Graphics, Japan*

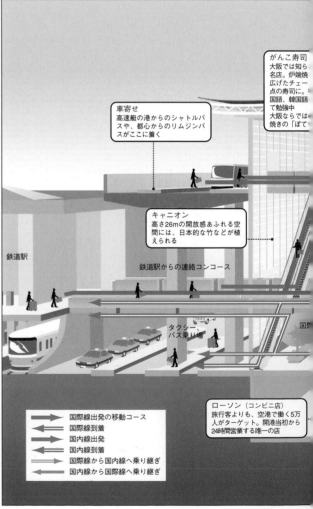

2

## 3
### EEC Import Quotas

A companion series to the
Spectrum scientific
encyclopaedia, the *Spectrum
Encyclopaedia of the World*,
was produced in ten volumes.
Illustrated here is a flow
diagram which describes
the free trade between the
then European Economic
Community and the European
Free Trade Association.
*Illustration: Mitchell Beazley
(ivr), U.K.; publisher: Spectrum,
The Netherlands*

3

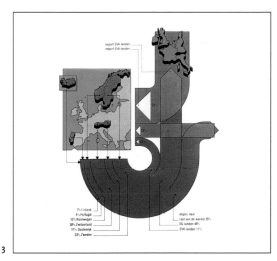

バーカウンター吉本
4階の両端2カ所に、あの吉本興
業がスタンドバーを出す。「お
笑い」は前面に出さないが、従
業員の制服や食器を吉本所属の
タレントにデザインさせ、さり
げなく「吉本」をアピール

ウイングシャトル
搭乗口とターミナルビル本館
の間を、3両編成で自動運行す
る。ウイングの先端駅まで1分
半。設計・据えつけ工事の国際
競争入札で、米国との間に政
治問題が生じた

**4階**

国際線出発フロア
国際線チェックインカウンター
セキュリティーチェック

**3階**
税関
出国手続き

飲食店・物販店フ

**2階**
国内線
チェックインカウンター
国内線出発・
到着フロア
検疫
入国手続き
国内線
ゲートラウンジ

税関 **1階**
国内線バゲージクレイム

国際線
バゲージクレイム

**地下1階**

ベルトコンベヤー（旅客手荷物処理システム）
4階で海外旅行客から受け取った手荷物を、仕分
けしながら1階へ降ろす。チェックインから仕分
けまで約10分。4階から1階までの高低差約14mは、
荷物が滑り落ちないように螺旋状のコンベヤーで
つなぐ

上の図は、南方からターミナルビルの■部分を見たところです

視点

*graphic by TUBE*

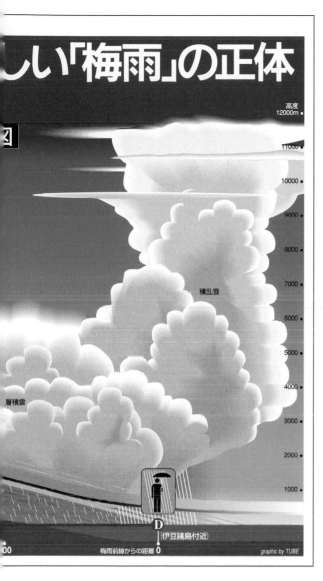

**1**

## Rainy Season in Japan

This diagram illustrates the natural forces at work during the rainy season in Japan, that is to say from June to the end of July. Consisting of a combination of a cross-section and a bird's-eye view of the country, the diagram shows cloud formations and weather fronts as they build over the Japan Sea, as well as the major cities of Tokyo and Niigata City and the Izu Islands in the Pacific Ocean.
*Design: Hiroyuki Kimura, Tube Graphics, Japan*

**2**

## Annual Global Energy Balance

This diagram, from a 1995 book entitled *Atmosphere, Climate and Change* written by Thomas E. Graedel and Paul J. Crutzen, explains the annual global energy balance of the Earth-Atmosphere System. Sensible heat is that which is transferred to the atmosphere from the earth's heated surface by means of turbulent eddies; latent heat is that which is supplied to the atmosphere through condensation. The numbers indicate percentages of energy derived from solar radiation.
*Publisher: Scientific American Library, U.S.A.*

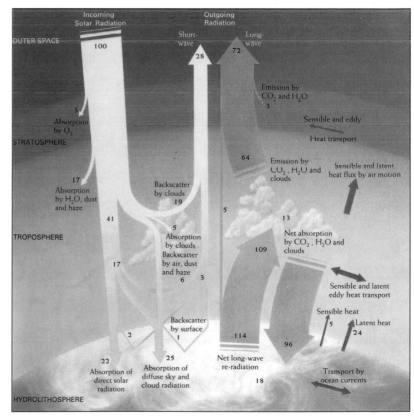

**2**

1 — 2

**Brochure Photomontages**

These two photomontages illustrating the causes of acid rain [1] and the effect of chemicals on the environment [2] are particularly good examples of the fusion of photographic and diagrammatic treatments to explain complex environmental problems and the linking of these to the page grid of a particular publication. Photomontage, a technique which dates back to the 1920s, is often employed to produce an effect greater than the sum of its component images. Although it is used less today, its place having been taken by the more innocuous collage or 'scrap-book' presentation, photomontage can be an effective and dramatic way of presenting a great deal of complex information.

*Design: Rosmarie Tissi, Odermatt & Tissi, Switzerland*

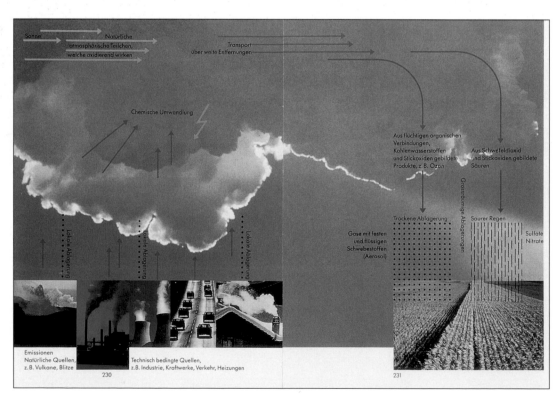

1

2

Recycling

Recycling (teilweise)

| Chemische Produktion | Produkte | Abfälle | Entsorgungsanlagen | Abluft |

Rohstoffe

Natur und Umwelt

| Rostoffverarbeitung | Güterproduktion | Konsumenten | Abfallentsorgung | Deponiegut | Deponie |

Recycling

Der Fortschritt in Wissenschaft und Technik und das wirtschaftliche Wachstum der letzten Jahrzehnte haben es mit sich gebracht, dass die Weltbevölkerung sprunghaft zugenommen und neue Lebensgewohnheiten angenommen hat. Sowohl die Herstellung und die Verteilung von Gütern als auch deren Verbrauch (Konsum) produzieren Berge von Abfall, Abwasser und Abluft. Es werden zudem die Rohstoffquellen übermässig beansprucht.

Diese Entwicklung hat dazu geführt, dass unsere Umwelt (Luft, Wasser, Boden) zunehmend verschmutzt und zum Teil überbeansprucht wird.

1

**The Death of the Family Farm**

2

**The Kobe Earthquake**

This diagram from *World Link*, the magazine of the World Economic Forum, illustrates the effects of AIDS on rural communities in Africa. Pictograms representing individual family members provide graphic impact.
*Design: Trevor Bounford and Associates, U.K.*

Created for the Associated Press, this diagram illustrates the Great Hamshin Earthquake, which shook the Japanese city of Kobe in January 1995. The diagram was updated on 19 January, two days after the quake, to incorporate information on the expansion of soil

liquefaction and was subsequently transmitted around the world. It shows in detail the number of victims by area and the locations of the active faults which caused this tragic event.
*Design: Hiroyuki Kimura, Tube Graphics, Japan*

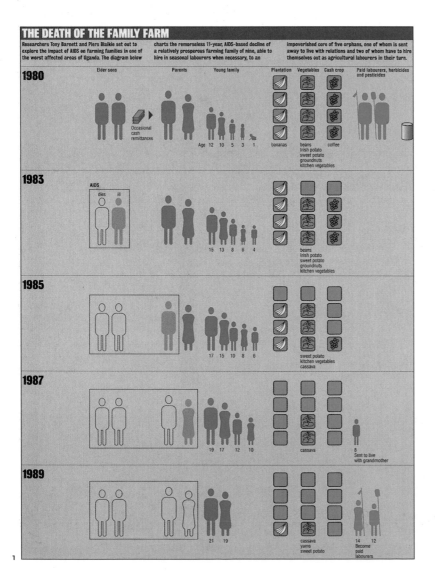

1

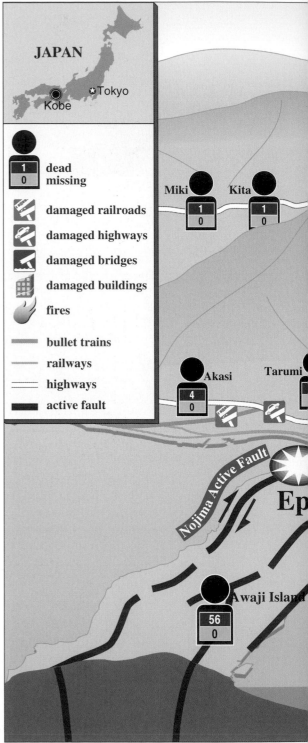

2

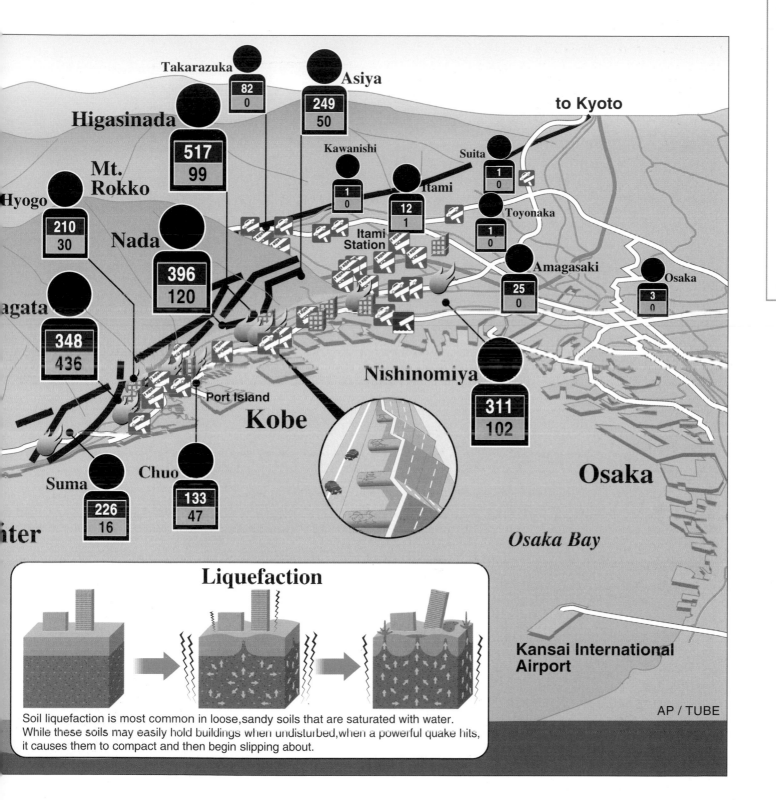

Takarazuka

82
0

Asiya

249
50

Higasinada

Kawanishi

Suita

to Kyoto

1
0

517
99

Mt.
Rokko

Itami

Hyogo

1
0

Itami
Station

12
1

Toyonaka

210
30

Nada

1
0

396
120

Amagasaki

Osaka

25
0

3
0

agata

348
436

Nishinomiya

311
102

Port Island

Kobe

Osaka

Suma

Chuo

226
16

133
47

ter

Osaka Bay

**Liquefaction**

Kansai International
Airport

Soil liquefaction is most common in loose, sandy soils that are saturated with water.
While these soils may easily hold buildings when undisturbed, when a powerful quake hits,
it causes them to compact and then begin slipping about.

AP / TUBE

# An ill wind

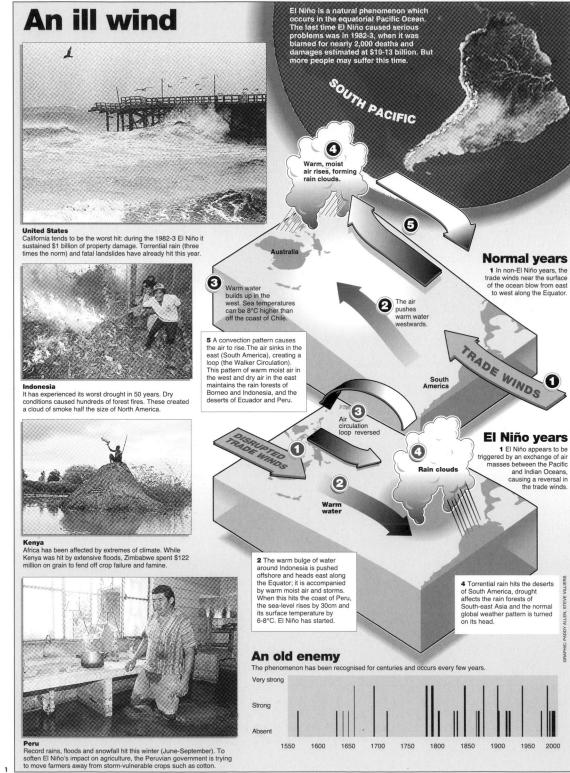

El Niño is a natural phenomenon which occurs in the equatorial Pacific Ocean. The last time El Niño caused serious problems was in 1982-3, when it was blamed for nearly 2,000 deaths and damages estimated at $10-13 billion. But more people may suffer this time.

**United States**
California tends to be the worst hit: during the 1982-3 El Niño it sustained $1 billion of property damage. Torrential rain (three times the norm) and fatal landslides have already hit this year.

**Indonesia**
It has experienced its worst drought in 50 years. Dry conditions caused hundreds of forest fires. These created a cloud of smoke half the size of North America.

**Kenya**
Africa has been affected by extremes of climate. While Kenya was hit by extensive floods, Zimbabwe spent $122 million on grain to fend off crop failure and famine.

**Peru**
Record rains, floods and snowfall hit this winter (June-September). To soften El Niño's impact on agriculture, the Peruvian government is trying to move farmers away from storm-vulnerable crops such as cotton.

SOUTH PACIFIC

**4** Warm, moist air rises, forming rain clouds.

Australia

**3** Warm water builds up in the west. Sea temperatures can be 8°C higher than off the coast of Chile.

**5** A convection pattern causes the air to rise. The air sinks in the east (South America), creating a loop (the Walker Circulation). This pattern of warm moist air in the west and dry air in the east maintains the rain forests of Borneo and Indonesia, and the deserts of Ecuador and Peru.

**2** The air pushes warm water westwards.

## Normal years
**1** In non-El Niño years, the trade winds near the surface of the ocean blow from east to west along the Equator.

TRADE WINDS

South America

DISRUPTED TRADE WINDS

**3** Air circulation loop reversed

**4** Rain clouds

**2** Warm water

## El Niño years
**1** El Niño appears to be triggered by an exchange of air masses between the Pacific and Indian Oceans, causing a reversal in the trade winds.

**2** The warm bulge of water around Indonesia is pushed offshore and heads east along the Equator; it is accompanied by warm moist air and storms. When this hits the coast of Peru, the sea-level rises by 30cm and its surface temperature by 6-8°C. El Niño has started.

**4** Torrential rain hits the deserts of South America, drought affects the rain forests of South-east Asia and the normal global weather pattern is turned on its head.

GRAPHIC: PADDY ALLEN, STEVE VILLIERS

## An old enemy
The phenomenon has been recognised for centuries and occurs every few years.

| | | |
|---|---|---|
| Very strong | | |
| Strong | | |
| Absent | | |

1550  1600  1650  1700  1750  1800  1850  1900  1950  2000

1

# Rebirthing canals

Containers designed for trucks can be carried on a new design of barge

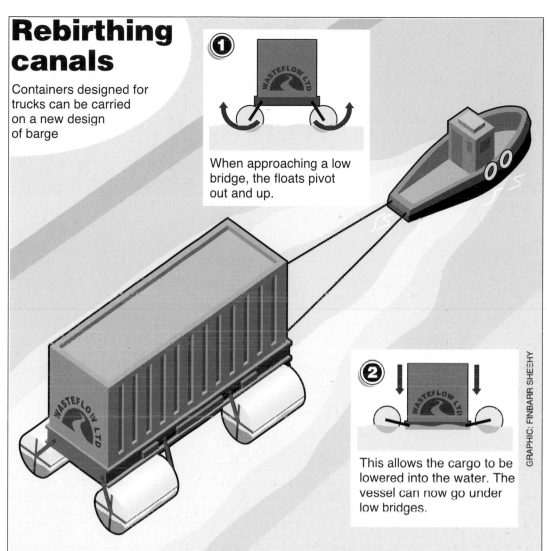

**①** When approaching a low bridge, the floats pivot out and up.

**②** This allows the cargo to be lowered into the water. The vessel can now go under low bridges.

GRAPHIC: FINBARR SHEEHY

2

1 — 2

**Newspaper Graphics**

Graphics like these from the *Guardian* newspaper, London, aim to explain the issues and facts behind current news stories and are always produced to very tight deadlines. The big 'analysis' graphics [1], which may take up a full page of the broadsheet, generally are the work of two or more people.

They start life as a layout which is broken down to be worked on by members of a team. By noon on a given day, the subject has been chosen by the editor and is usually based on a topic which will gain through a graphical approach. A researcher collects all the relevant data for the graphics team, which

works closely with the page designer. Roughs are agreed and first proofs are ready for checking by late afternoon. Detailed drawing continues and last proofs are checked and finished artwork delivered that same evening. *Design: Paddy Allen and Steve Villiers [1]; Finbarr Sheehy [2].*

# Rolls Royce Aerospace CD-ROM
## Creating a Prototype Cinegram

This case study describes one product of work carried out at Coventry University within a research programme entitled 'Online Multimedia Information for Maintenance and Operation' (OMIMO). This programme, funded by the European Union, was conducted in collaboration with a number of industrial and research organizations throughout Europe, including Rolls Royce. The product is a multimedia prototype technical document for which the term 'cinegram' was coined. The cinegram is an interactive systems diagram through which a user can navigate to call up texts, photographs and, significantly, animated diagrammatic sequences.

Where the initial move to digital media has taken place in an industrial context, this has typically been by a process of transposing a pre-existing book structure into a computer-based format. The creation of the cinegram involved taking advantage of characteristics which digital technology has and books do not, resulting in a new kind of information resource. The basic component of the book is usually a text. The text provides signposts to other information resources,

1

The animated overview of components.

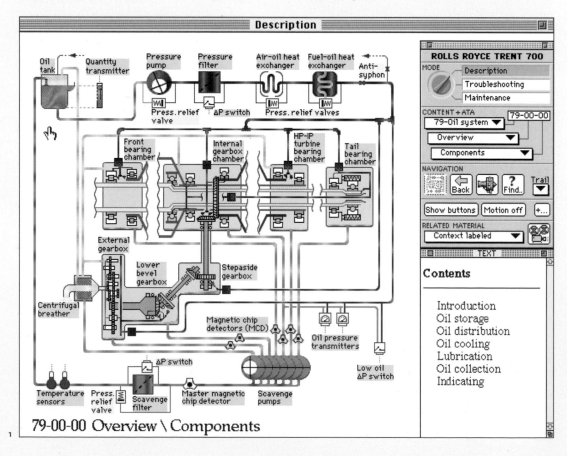

such as diagrams, which are embedded within it and which are generally accessed through it. We have experimented with the opposite approach, where the starting point of an interactive document is an overview diagram which acts as a kind of graphical index to a range of visual information resources.

Working in collaboration with Rolls Royce, we developed a prototype cinegram for the oil system of the Trent turbofan aeroengine. The introductory overview was based on an existing paper-based diagram called an Engineering Technical Graphic (ETG). The ETG of the Trent oil system was chosen because of its diagrammatic richness and popularity within Rolls Royce as a multipurpose reference document.

The cinegram overview diagram differs from the ETG in very significant ways. Firstly, the layout was re-organized to emphasize functional relationships at the expense of literal spatial ones. Secondly, the flow of oil around the system was made explicit by means of palette cycling. Thirdly, there is a navigation control panel situated at the right-hand side of all screens below which is a scrolling text box. Fourthly, the overview (and other diagrams) have hot spots at key points onto which the user can click by means of a cursor.

With these last two features, a user can navigate through the extensive, hierarchically arranged information resource which can be used to explore the oil system and its operation. For example, users can navigate from a component representation on the overview diagram to a more detailed diagrammatic presentation of that component

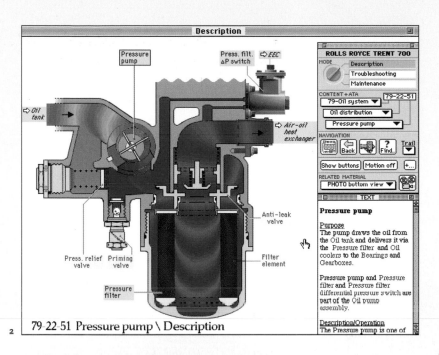

2

79-22-51 Pressure pump \ Description

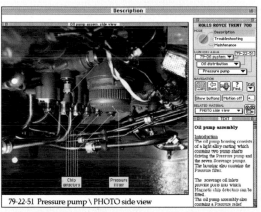

3   79-22-51 Pressure pump \ PHOTO side view

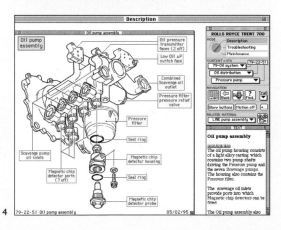

4   79-22-51 Oil pump assembly     05/02/95

2

The pressure pump is shown in detail.

3 – 4

These screens show a photograph and an outline drawing of the oil-pump assembly.

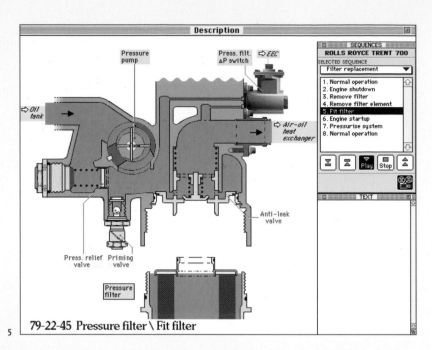

5

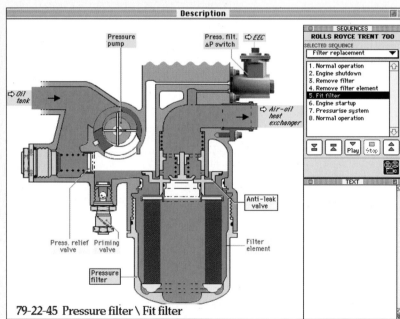

6

box displays related reading matter [3–4].

The cinegram prototype was developed over a two-year period through an integrated process of field research, design, implementation and formative evaluation. As a consequence of this approach, the structure and scope of the cinegram changed a number of times. Originally, the idea had been limited to a relatively self-contained application for the oil system. Later on, the concept developed of a modular architecture which could accommodate cinegrams dealing with other engine systems.

A study of existing technical publications highlighted the need to consider how updating might be carried out and how interfacing to other computer systems could be achieved. Also identified was the potential usefulness of being able to customize the cinegram for different categories of application and to correspond to users' preferred approaches to using its information resources.

HyperCard™ by Apple was chosen to implement the prototype. Whilst the chosen architecture was sufficient to demonstrate the validity of the cinegram concept, a more fundamental reworking behind the scenes would be necessary to produce a sufficiently robust and adaptable system for effective commercial use in an industrial context.

One of the cinegram's major features is animation [5–6]. Three types of dynamic presentation can be distinguished: steady-state, state-change and sequence.

Steady-state animation uses a refined version of colour cycling and produces an effect similar to the interference patterns created by rotating wheels behind the partially transparent display panels used for depicting power plants. In the cinegram, this technique indicates flow type, direction and speed. In static, printed displays, this information would be inferred from some

5 – 6

Two frames from an animation sequence show the filter pump's re-assembly.

[1–2]. This itself may be activated to show, say, animations of different flow rates under various operating conditions, or the disassembling of a component. Other screens use photographs and outline drawings to show the appearance and locations of components while the text

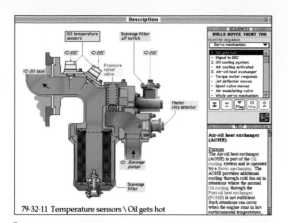

**79-32-11 Temperature sensors \ Oil gets hot**

7

**79-32-11 Temperature sensors \ Overheat warning**

8

**79-21-00 Oil cooling 3**

9

**79-21-51 Air-oil heat exchanger \ Description**

10

7 – 8

Additional screens show how temperature sensors detect overheating and generate a warning.

9 – 10

Other diagrams include information on the maintenance of the oil-cooling mechanism and a description of the air-oil heat exchanger.

form of symbolic coding (e.g., directional arrows).

State-changes are shown by linking two steady-state animation segments, with one or more transitional segments. On completion, each segment calls up the subsequent one until the final state is reached. This approach can be used to depict different sorts of activity. Exceptional conditions may be shown, such as a filter becoming blocked by a build-up of debris from elsewhere in the engine system. State-change can also be used to redirect attention to a particular component or process.

Sequences combine any number of animation segments, which may be played as a whole, stepped through or accessed arbitrarily by using the control panel. The scripting for each sequence essentially comprises a list which points to the requisite 'trigger' for each animation segment. The same animation segment can therefore be utilized in various different sequences.

Digital diagrammatics of the sort used in the cinegram are going to play an increasingly important role by providing valuable resources for learners and experts alike. The cinegram described here was produced by a process of adapting printed matter from existing technical documents, modifying engineering production drawings and creating entirely new diagrammatic material. In the future, cinegrams may be produced more economically by re-using the computer-aided design data which defines the engineering components represented.          *Clive Richards*

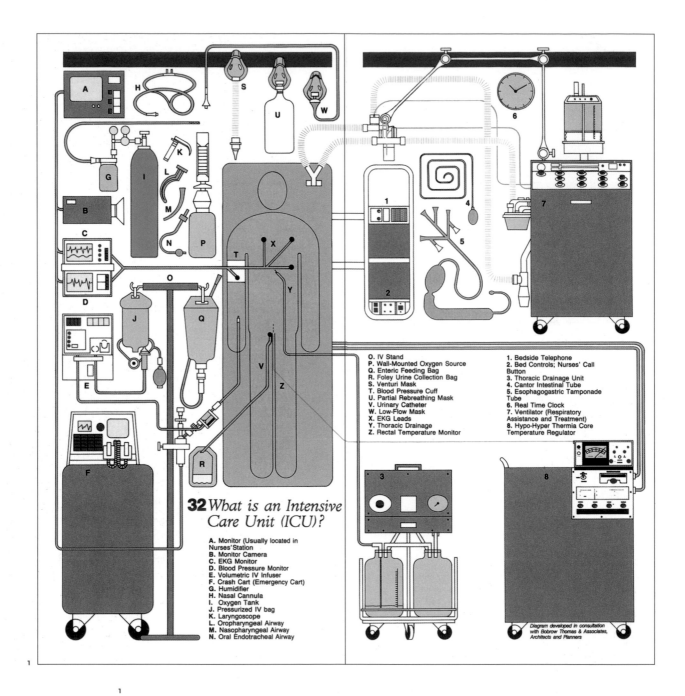

**32** *What is an Intensive Care Unit (ICU)?*

A. Monitor (Usually located in Nurses' Station
B. Monitor Camera
C. EKG Monitor
D. Blood Pressure Monitor
E. Volumetric IV Infuser
F. Crash Cart (Emergency Cart)
G. Humidifier
H. Nasal Cannula
I. Oxygen Tank
J. Pressurized IV bag
K. Laryngoscope
L. Oropharyngeal Airway
M. Nasopharyngeal Airway
N. Oral Endotracheal Airway

O. IV Stand
P. Wall-Mounted Oxygen Source
Q. Enteric Feeding Bag
R. Foley Urine Collection Bag
S. Venturi Mask
T. Blood Pressure Cuff
U. Partial Rebreathing Mask
V. Urinary Catheter
W. Low-Flow Mask
X. EKG Leads
Y. Thoracic Drainage
Z. Rectal Temperature Monitor

1. Bedside Telephone
2. Bed Controls; Nurses' Call Button
3. Thoracic Drainage Unit
4. Cantor Intestinal Tube
5. Esophagogastric Tamponade Tube
6. Real Time Clock
7. Ventilator (Respiratory Assistance and Treatment)
8. Hypo-Hyper Thermia Core Temperature Regulator

*Diagram developed in consultation with Bobrow Thomas & Associates, Architects and Planners*

1

*Medical Access*

Many design projects evolve through personal experience; this book is no exception. While preparing himself for a medical examination, the book's designer, Richard Saul Wurman, failed to find adequate information upon which to base the questions he thought he should ask. This was the starting point for *Medical Access*. The book is broken down into three basic sections: explanations of 120 diagnostic tests [2]; surgical procedures, including preparation, procedures and recovery; and questions and answers [1].

*Concept: Richard Saul Wurman, U.S.A.; diagrams: Michael Everitt, Lorraine Christiani, U.S.A.*

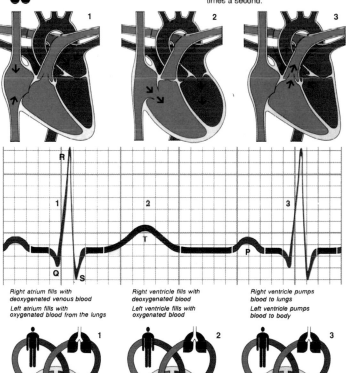

**ELECTROCARDIOGRAM** *ECG, CARDIOGRAM, EKG, 12-LEAD EKG, HOLTER MONITOR*

**Like a car engine, the heart depends on electrical energy to start it and keep it beating regularly. This energy is generated by the body's own**

pacemaker, a tiny bundle of nerve fibers called the *sinoatrial (SA) node*, which is located in the upper right chamber or atrium of the heart. In a healthy heart, the impulse follows a strict rhythmic pattern. The impulse is fired and sends an electric wave to the 2 upper chambers, the atria. They contract and force the blood into the larger lower chambers, the ventricles.

The wave of electricity then moves to the *atrioventricular (AV) node*, the junction where the signal is split and conducted to the 2 ventricles; the ventricles contract and pump blood to the lungs and the body. There is a brief period of relaxation as the atria fill with returning blood and the SA node prepares to fire again. Then the whole process is repeated—usually about 2 times a second.

*Right atrium fills with deoxygenated venous blood*

*Left atrium fills with oxygenated blood from the lungs*

*Right ventricle fills with deoxygenated blood*

*Left ventricle fills with oxygenated blood*

*Right ventricle pumps blood to lungs*

*Left ventricle pumps blood to body*

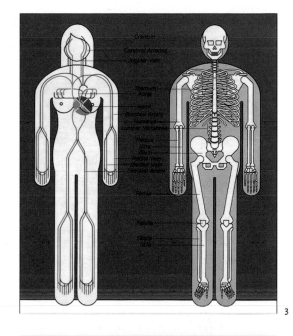

3

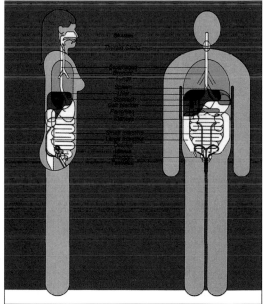

4

**2 – 4**
*Medical Access*

The design of the book is extremely graphic, utilizing colour coding, a range of pictograms and highly structured typography.

The comprehensive range of schematic diagrams using layering techniques is exemplary.

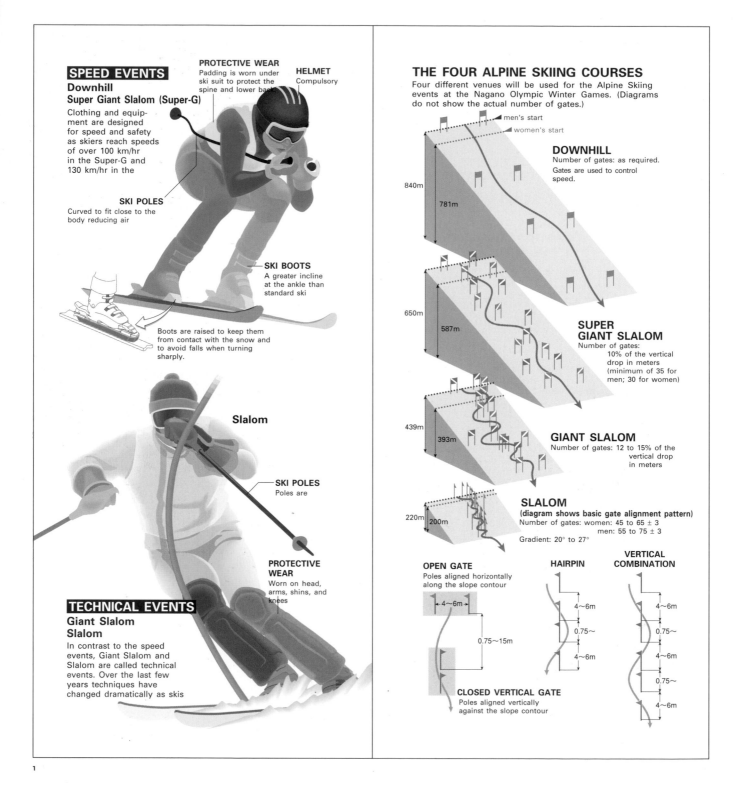

## SPEED EVENTS
### Downhill
### Super Giant Slalom (Super-G)

Clothing and equipment are designed for speed and safety as skiers reach speeds of over 100 km/hr in the Super-G and 130 km/hr in the

**PROTECTIVE WEAR**
Padding is worn under ski suit to protect the spine and lower back

**HELMET**
Compulsory

**SKI POLES**
Curved to fit close to the body reducing air

**SKI BOOTS**
A greater incline at the ankle than standard ski

Boots are raised to keep them from contact with the snow and to avoid falls when turning sharply.

### Slalom

**SKI POLES**
Poles are

**PROTECTIVE WEAR**
Worn on head, arms, shins, and knees

## TECHNICAL EVENTS
### Giant Slalom
### Slalom

In contrast to the speed events, Giant Slalom and Slalom are called technical events. Over the last few years techniques have changed dramatically as skis

## THE FOUR ALPINE SKIING COURSES

Four different venues will be used for the Alpine Skiing events at the Nagano Olympic Winter Games. (Diagrams do not show the actual number of gates.)

men's start
women's start

**DOWNHILL**
Number of gates: as required.
Gates are used to control speed.

840m
781m

**SUPER GIANT SLALOM**
Number of gates:
10% of the vertical drop in meters (minimum of 35 for men; 30 for women)

650m
587m

**GIANT SLALOM**
Number of gates: 12 to 15% of the vertical drop in meters

439m
393m

**SLALOM**
(diagram shows basic gate alignment pattern)
Number of gates: women: 45 to 65 ± 3
men: 55 to 75 ± 3
Gradient: 20° to 27°

220m
200m

**OPEN GATE**
Poles aligned horizontally along the slope contour

4~6m
0.75~15m

**CLOSED VERTICAL GATE**
Poles aligned vertically against the slope contour

**HAIRPIN**
4~6m
0.75~
4~6m

**VERTICAL COMBINATION**
4~6m
0.75~
4~6m
0.75~
4~6m

*Nagano Winter Olympics Guide Book*

These two spreads from the official guide for the 1998 Winter Olympic Games in Japan deal with Alpine skiing [1] and ice hockey [2]. The skiing spread outlines the differences between downhill, super-giant slalom, giant slalom and slalom. The left-hand page describes the clothing and equipment used for speed and technical events – for example, ski types, poles and body protectors – and the right-hand page explains the various courses/venues together with the technical aspects of the courses such as the positioning of poles and the intervals between them. Like skiers, hockey players require protective clothing, which in the case of goalkeepers is quite complicated. Here, the various components are outlined along with fouls and regulations.
*Design: Hiroyuki Kimura, Tube Graphics, Japan*

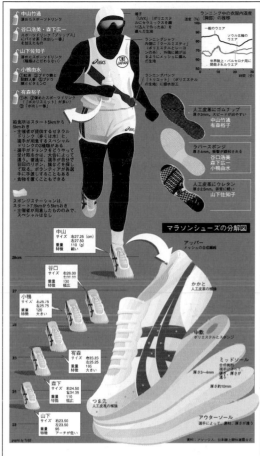

3

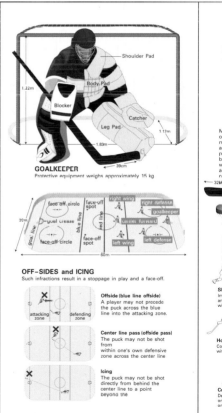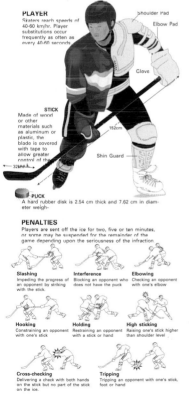

2

**3**
**Marathon Runners and Shoes**

This diagram illustrates and describes the various types of running shoes and their construction, as well as the preferences of individual competitors in the Barcelona Olympics Marathon of 1992.
*Design: Hiroyuki Kimura, Tube Graphics, Japan*

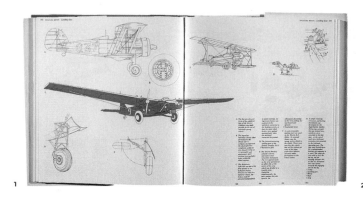

1

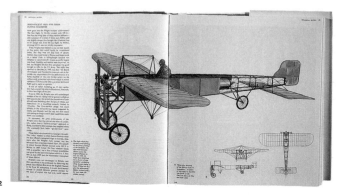

2

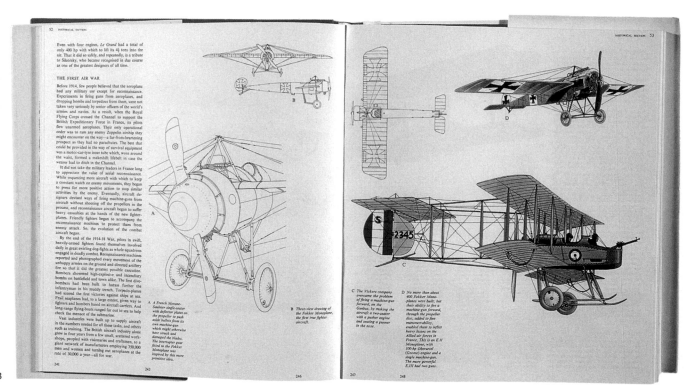

3

1 – 6
**Nordbok Publications**

Produced since the 1960s, this series of books has been continuously revised and extended. The individual volumes deal with a variety of technical subjects, including trains, ships, machines and so on.

The books could be described as technical encyclopaedias in the tradition of Diderot's famous eighteenth-century French compendia. They are well researched and have a sophisticated visual system of detailed drawings and diagrams. Illustrated here are spreads from two Nordbok classics, *Lore of Flight* [1 – 3] and *The Camera* [3 – 6].
*Publisher: Nordbok, Sweden*

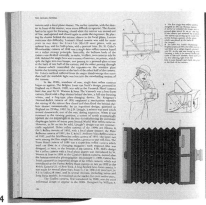

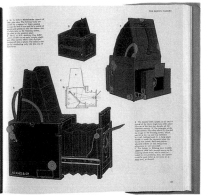

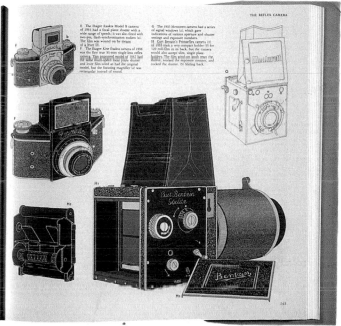

1 — 2

**Felco Technical Guide**

Felco is a Swiss company specializing in the manufacture of high-quality pruning shears and wire cutters. This page [1] taken from their technical brochure mainly uses line drawings [2] and a simple storyboard treatment to clearly convey the sequence of actions necessary to replace cutter blades.

*Design and text: Felco sa and Synergetique sa, Switzerland; drawings: B Leu Graphic Design, Switzerland; photos: Degen Jacques*

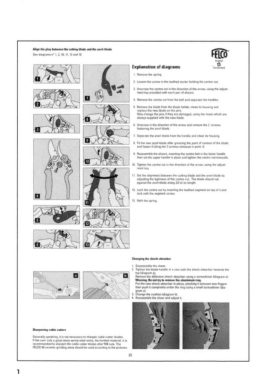

1

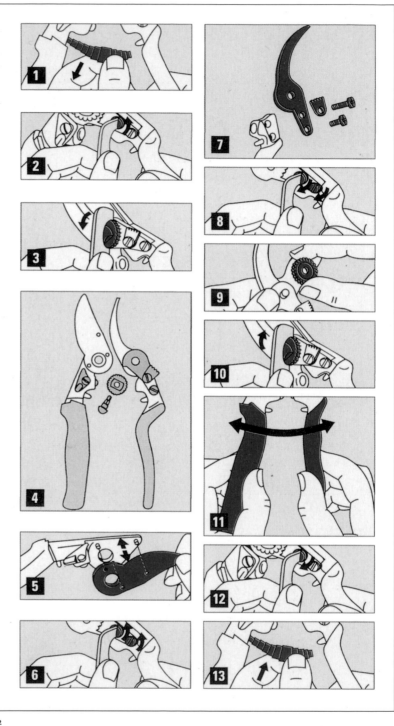

2

### Knowing where to locate your vending machine

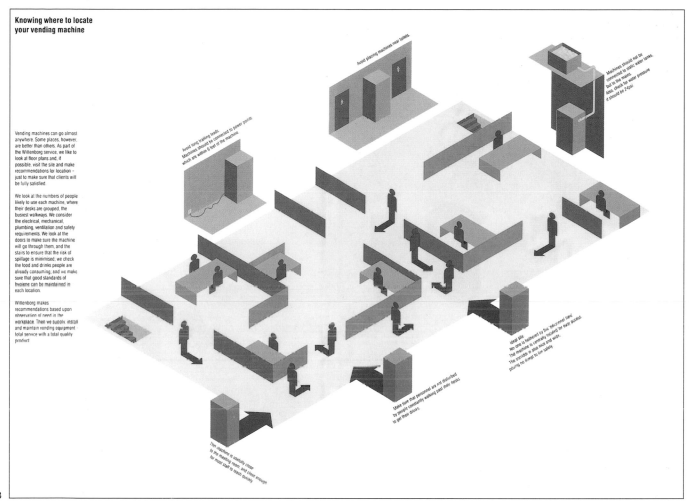

Vending machines can go almost anywhere. Some places, however, are better than others. As part of the Wittenborg service, we like to look at floor plans and, if possible, visit the site and make recommendations for location – just to make sure that clients will be fully satisfied.

We look at the numbers of people likely to use each machine, where their desks are grouped, the busiest walkways. We consider the electrical, mechanical, plumbing, ventilation and safety requirements. We look at the doors to make sure the machine will go through them, and the stairs to ensure that the risk of spillage is minimised; we check the food and drinks people are already consuming; and we make sure that good standards of hygiene can be maintained in each location.

Wittenborg makes recommendations based upon observation of need in the workplace. Then we supply, install and maintain vending equipment – total service with a total quality product.

**3**

## Installing a Vending Machine

This spread from a technical brochure describes the range of products, positioning and setting up of Wittenborg (U.K.) vending machines. The illustration indicates some of the ways in which these machines can be integrated both functionally and aesthetically and is directed at the architect and specifier. Another dimension to the planning process involves minimizing the time lost in walking to a particular machine.
*Design: Minds Eye, U.K.; illustration: Craig Austin, U.K.*

1

**1 – 3**
IBM **Thinkpad Assembly Instructions**

The original packaging and user manuals of the IBM Thinkpad™ laptop computers did not mirror the product's sophisticated technology. IBM asked the designers to analyze the problem and provide new design solutions. They found that the most critical experience for the buyer is the first contact with the expensive, newly purchased product: unpacking the shipping box and assembling the computer at home or in the office.

To enhance this experience, the designers created a poster-size product map [1–2] which, packaged together with the computer, orientates the user in the initial assembly. Once the user has placed each computer component on the corresponding area of the map, the step-by-step assembly process becomes obvious [3].
*Design: Krzysztof Lenk,
Dynamic Diagrams,
U.S.A.*

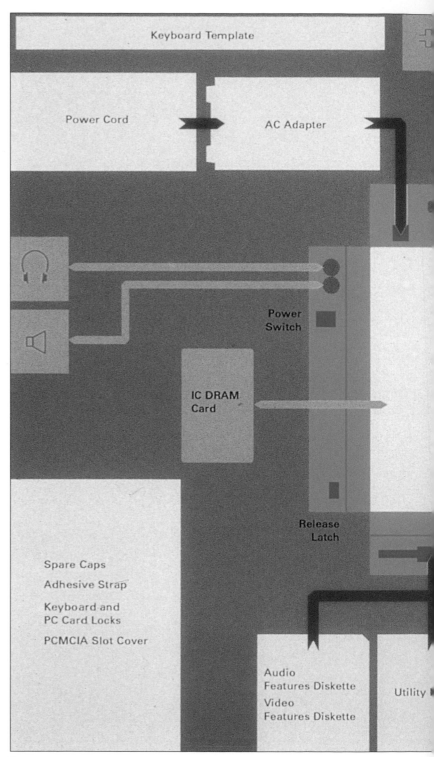

Keyboard Template

Power Cord

AC Adapter

Power
Switch

IC DRAM
Card

Release
Latch

Spare Caps

Adhesive Strap

Keyboard and
PC Card Locks

PCMCIA Slot Cover

Audio
Features Diskette
Video
Features Diskette

Utility

2

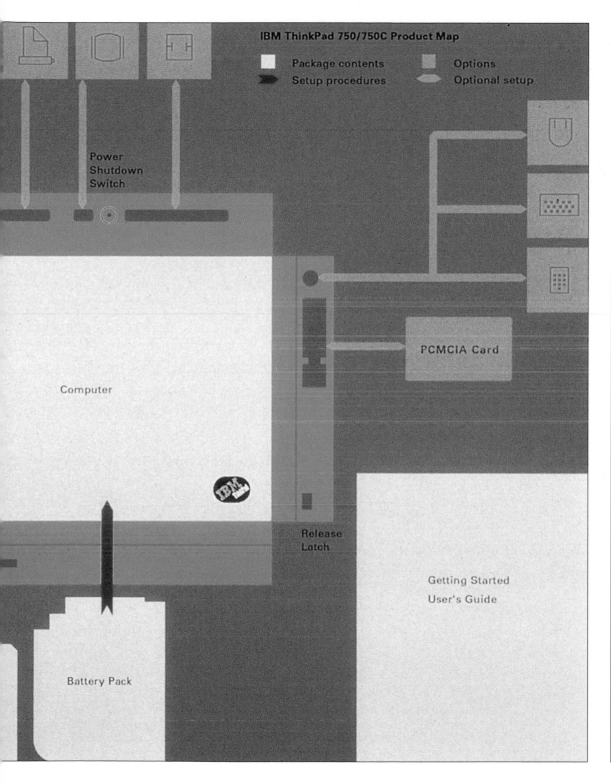

## IBM ThinkPad 750/750C Product Map

- ☐ Package contents
- ► Setup procedures
- ☐ Options
- ⬭ Optional setup

Power Shutdown Switch

Computer

PCMCIA Card

Release Latch

Battery Pack

Getting Started
User's Guide

3

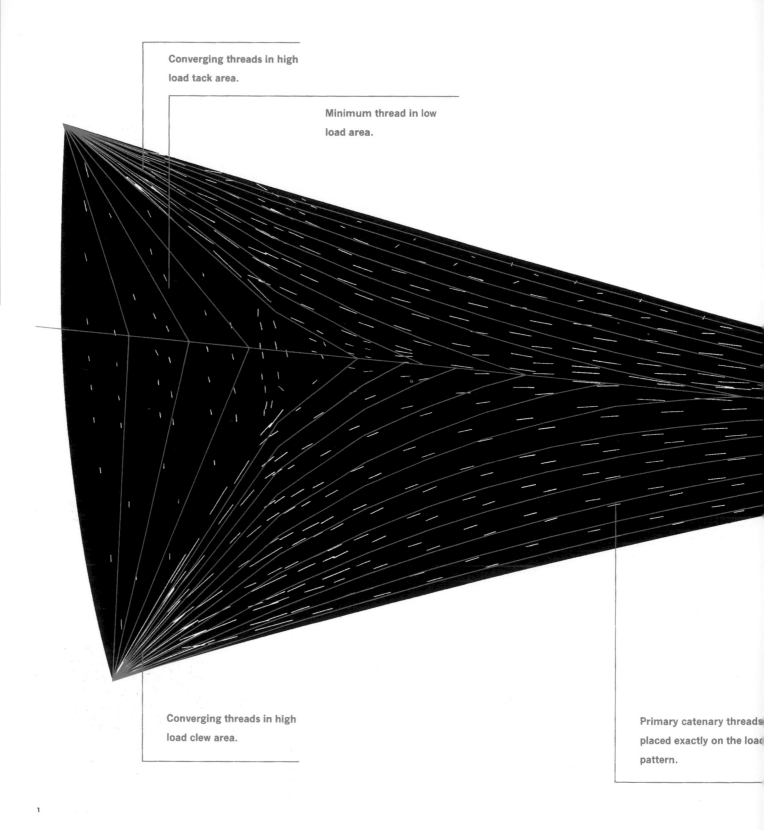

Converging threads in high
load tack area.

Minimum thread in low
load area.

Converging threads in high
load clew area.

Primary catenary threads
placed exactly on the load
pattern.

1

**1 — 2**
**'Genesis' Sails**

These illustrations are taken from a brochure about high-performance yacht sails produced by the Sobstad Corporation in the United States. The company's design process begins with a detailed study of the stresses and aerodynamic forces acting on a sail [1] so that they can manufacture an integrated, load-related structure to provide greater efficiency and durability than more conventional sails. This procedure involves using a range of moulding and laminating techniques [2] and synthetic materials such as polyester, Kevlar and Mylar.
*Design: Pocknell Studio, U.K.*

**Converging threads in high load head area.**

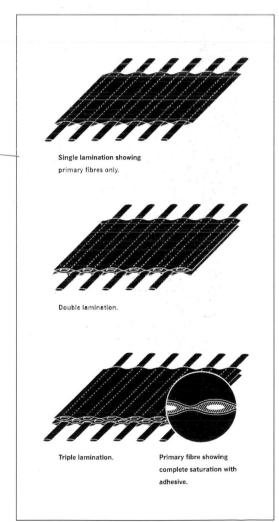

Single lamination showing primary fibres only.

Double lamination.

Triple lamination.

Primary fibre showing complete saturation with adhesive.

2

# 3 Controlling the Input

Cockpit Design • Digital Control Panels

The information designer has an important role to play at the front end of the product-design process, particularly in the area which can be described as the interface between user and machine. Product design is very much a team effort with representation being based on the nature of the technology employed. It may involve major input from engineers or electronic specialists, but in almost every case will involve a product designer, ergonomist and interface designer.

There are several important differences between interfaces which were used before the introduction of electronics and those that followed it. These differences had to do with the nature of the product/machine, which had typically evolved over a period of time and which, in the main, had been designed to carry out only one function. It was generally agreed at that time that products which tried to fulfil two or more functions were

compromises and therefore inferior to a single-function product. A further factor was that the operation of the machine was governed by simple mechanical principles which were usually obvious or intuitive for the operator. With the advent of electronics (transistors, integrated circuits and sensors), the situation changed quite rapidly, although the two concepts existed side by side for a while as, for example, in washing machines of the mid-1980s. Products and machines became capable of being used in a variety of modes (again, the history of the washing machine illustrates this general tendency with a proliferation of programs and user choices), and this new, extended use required either training or a detailed study of an instruction manual in order to master it. This new range of functions and a largely opaque technology radically altered the nature and complexity of the interface.

The interface is that part of a design with which the user first comes into contact and through which he or she experiences both its capabilities and the ease (or otherwise) of its operation. There are many examples of basically sound products which are let down by either an off-putting initial impression or the continued irritation they cause through minor faults in the placing or labelling of controls. To a certain extent, these faults can be rectified by sensible testing procedures, but some shortcomings can only be changed by expensive redesign. The best solution, and often the most economical one, is to employ an information designer at the beginning of a project, when changes can be made more easily. Information design is often viewed as merely providing a cosmetic contribution to a product, a contribution which goes no deeper than the product's casing. This is a misunderstanding of the designer's role. Our definition would be a much wider one and would include the disposition of all input controls such as switches, knobs or buttons, their grouping and identification, as well as any feed-back mechanisms such as dials or warning lights.

Surprisingly few product manufacturers retain the services of a designer with typographic experience or attach any significance to the detailed considerations of the lettering which will appear on a new product. A large proportion of products suffer as a result from inappropriate or faddish letter forms, the manufacturer forgetting that the whole functionality and efficiency of the product may be judged on the evidence of this one detail. The designer's role in the annotating of controls involves making informed decisions about the choice of letter forms/type-faces, hierarchies of use, choice of lower-case or capitals and the positioning of words in a consistent way in relation to each control. Similar considerations apply to the letter forms and graphics used on any input/output display.

The use of pictograms – pictorial graphic equivalents of a function or action – is widely seen as a more satisfactory alternative to using words because pictograms do not require translation into other languages. Unfortunately, they are not a universal solution for cultural and other reasons. Pictograms are most sucessful when they are used to represent an easily recognized object and this meaning can be extended to convey a larger idea, depending on the context. The vocabulary of pictograms includes a negative symbol (a diagonal bar placed over the symbol), but in general pictograms are not practical for expressing abstract concepts.

Developments in the practical techniques of applying typographic and pictographic information to a product have progressed to the state where lettering need no longer be applied with a separate backing material. Individual characters can now be applied directly to almost any flat or curved surface. In the case of moulded products, the information can often be incorporated into the mould or die during the production process.

Out of the wide spectrum of objects requiring interfaces that ranges from the personal hand-held product to the large-scale command centre, we will consider three: the hand-held device, the road vehicle and the aircraft cockpit.

The interface of a hand-held product presents a number of design problems. Because of its small size and portability, the power source is most often a battery. This implies a low-resolution screen which probably uses segmented alphanumeric characters and limited graphics. A small screen limits the number of lines of text appearing without scrolling, and internal lighting may not be an option. Small dimensions also mean that buttons cannot be allocated on the basis of one per function; some controls have to work in several modes, a problem most of us are familiar with on the constricted scale of digital watches. This can lead to confusion if there is no way of indicating the current mode of operation. Since many portable products are designed to be used out-of-doors, there are additional problems of cold (which might affect the power supply) and waterproofing. Outdoor operators wearing gloves cannot easily deal with small buttons, recessed controls or buttons set too close to each other.

In addition to these constraints, which can act as challenges as well as problems, there is a range of issues to be addressed in the area of products for the disabled, particularly the blind (see pp. 140–43). Solutions to these challenges can produce superior designs for everyone. Products which capture the public imagination, such as mobile phones, also provide opportunities which can lead to optimal solutions.

In the early days of vehicle design, there was very little thought given to the matching of the interface with human abilities and almost none given to compensating for variations in the size, height and grip of human operators. It was expected that the user would learn to 'fit' the machine rather than the other way round. In terms of the layout of instruments, there were often good reasons for this approach, since speeds were generally lower, the roads were clearer, and users had more time to look at instruments. There was also a more direct relationship between user and power source; in cars with manual transmissions, the driver's senses were attuned to the sounds and vibrations of the engine and gear-box, and so instruments were not the primary sources of information that they have become today.

A number of factors led to the ergonomic designs which we find in almost all mass-produced vehicles today. First was the demand for an increasing number of ancillary controls, originally installed as luxury extras. All of these controls had to be placed within easy reach and sight of the driver. To save space, vehicle makers initially reduced the number of instrument dials conveying secondary information and replaced them with warning lights, but then two industrial developments helped to solve the problem of crowding and potential confusion. A number of previously separate instruments were grouped together within a common housing. In addition, the development of moulded plastics to produce ergonomic dashboards enabled instruments to be angled towards the driver to ensure maximum visibility. The flexibility of plastics technology also suggested the concept of consoles forming natural groupings of related instruments.

The introduction of early forms of digital instrumentation and its relatively low cost compared with mechanical instrumentation led to an overuse of numerical displays. At some time or other, almost every type of vehicle instrument was replaced by a digital/numerical equivalent using illuminated digits or a back-lit display. However, most drivers resisted these numerical versions, partly because of the difficulty of converting from one system to another, but mainly because human beings seem to prefer the benefits of the analogue 'context' within which decisions are easier to make. Analogue, or digitally simulated analogue, controls have now become standard for the major instruments on most vehicles.

The cockpit of a single-seat aircraft or the flight deck of a huge airliner presents a critical environment in which a pilot has to make judgements in response to an even greater number of inputs and systems and has to have absolute confidence in the information given by his or her instruments. This is particularly true in conditions in which information based on observation is non-existent or even contradictory.

The most critical instrument for the pilot is the altimeter, and any misreading or misinterpretation of the height of an aircraft can have disasterous consequences. As with road vehicles, attempts were made to replace the mechanical analogue instruments, including the long-established analogue altimeter, with purely numerical displays. But after a number of accidents which were presumed to have been caused by misinterpretation of the digital version, the analogue one returned, combined with a small numerical sub-display providing the best of both formats. One of the problems of the purely numerical display was that in conditions of rapid height loss, it was difficult to interpret the rate of change. The other problem associated with all-numerical displays is that they require analysis, which takes time. Normally, this is of no consequence, but in critical situations such time delays can lead to accidents.

Digital colour displays in the most appropriate graphic format can now provide unlimited information to a pilot on the functioning of any one of an aircraft's numerous systems. The design problem lies in prioritizing the essential information and assigning a scale of importance to the warning devices. There also must be a degree of standardization in the interface formats and procedures which appear in similar types of aircraft, just as there is in vehicle interface design, so that control and instrumentation familiarization between aircraft become simple and straightforward procedures.

1

## 1 – 3
**Dornier 328 Cockpit Layout**

Passenger aircraft design has changed beyond all recognition during the last seventy years. Nonetheless, a pilot from the 1920s or '30s would feel right at home with the general layout and grouping of instruments found in contemporary airliners, since tradition and a multitude of regulations have restricted new developments in design. There have been exceptions, however. This model from the German aircraft manufacturer Dornier illustrates clearly what can be achieved. The Dornier 328 cockpit design was carried out at full size and illustrates the cockpit as a complete workplace. Great attention was paid to ergonomics, to interaction between controls and to instruments which traditionally were individually mounted. Essential instruments were grouped together on computer screens. The overall impression is one of considered cohesiveness.
*Design: Peter Burgeff, Germany*

2

# Air Traffic Control Screens
## Choosing Colour Palettes for Layered Information

A typical monochrome display [1] and a typical background map in monochrome [2].

Air traffic controllers work with computerized radar displays on which the position of each aircraft is shown by means of a symbol and a label. The aircraft positions are updated every few seconds. There is also a background map mainly consisting of boundary lines representing divisions of airspace, some of which overlap one another. In the past, these displays were shown in monochrome, usually green on a black background [1–2]. Now, however, they are being replaced by high-resolution colour displays in many air traffic control (ATC) centres, usually on the assumption that colour will help in the presentation of more complex data than was shown on the traditional display, thus enhancing controllers' performance.

Early examples of coloured ATC displays have differently coloured lines and symbols on a dark background. However, this approach does not realize the full potential of either the display technology or colour itself, given the possibility of using differently coloured, infilled backgrounds. Also, unsuitable choices of colours could lead to misperception of data and/or visual fatigue.

National Air Traffic Services Ltd (NATS) felt that the best way of ensuring the appropriate use of colour on U.K. ATC displays would be to draw up a draft colour standard for use by display designers. They therefore initiated and funded research and development work which was undertaken by a Colour Group set up within the NATS Research and Development Directorate. Group members included civil controllers, a military controller, a scientist, a psychologist and human factors specialist and myself as a colour specialist.

When colour first becomes available for displays such as these, the first thought is often to use it for colour coding. But this is not the only way of using colour. On a typical monochrome ATC radar display, the background map and foreground

1

2

data have much the same visual emphasis. The Colour Group felt that a clearer difference between background and foreground could reduce the controller's information processing load, so it was suggested that the display should be thought of as a series of conceptual 'layers' differing in importance, and that colour should be used primarily to represent these as a series of visual layers, with the foreground data having the greatest visual emphasis and the background map the least. It was agreed that a facility for colour coding the moving foreground data could be useful, and that the displays should be visually restful and capable of being used in normal office lighting. Such displays might then offer the possibility of more efficient working with more complex data than in the past, and a consequent increase in the number of aircraft that could be handled.

It soon became clear to the Colour Group that it would not be practicable to specify a fixed set of colours for every kind of ATC display. What was needed was a set of carefully selected palettes corresponding to the conceptual layers the Group had identified. The display designer would first sort the objects to be displayed into conceptual layers and then choose colours from the appropriate palettes. This would give flexibility whilst minimizing the likelihood of colour problems. As the colour specialist, my brief was to develop these colour palettes, together with guidelines for their use, and to produce prototype full-colour radar displays in static form.

I began by carrying out a thorough survey of

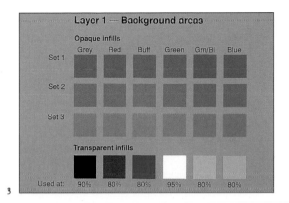

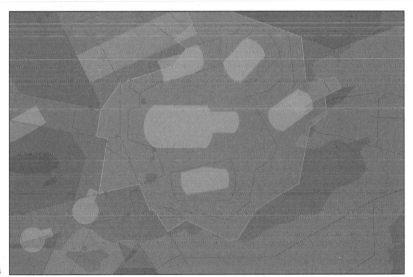

the research literature on a variety of topics including mapping techniques, the psychology of colour coding, colour perception, the physiology of colour vision, the use of colour displays and the effects of ambient lighting. This process took several months, and I did not begin to create the palettes or any prototype displays until it was completed.

Among the conclusions I drew from this survey were the following:

3 – 4

The background palettes [3] and the same map shown in [2] in colour [4].

A typical display using the NATS colour palettes [5] and the foreground palettes [6].

• A grey background of medium luminance would enhance perception of colour in the foreground, would be visually restful and would allow the displays to be used in normal office lighting.

• The colour dimensions of luminance, saturation and hue could be systematically manipulated to create the visual layering required and to reflect the logical relationships between foreground data items.

• The use of transparent layers of colour was likely to be an appropriate technique for showing overlapping background areas.

• In devising colour palettes for the foreground layers, it would be important to take into account the ease of discriminating between colours and their effect on the legibility of the aircraft labels.

• The number of highly saturated colours and the area they occupied on the display would need to be kept to a minimum so as to avoid colour illusions and visual fatigue.

These conclusions led to the palettes illustrated here [3, 6]. Prototype displays were then created using FreeHand on a Macintosh computer. I found FreeHand particularly suitable because of the ease of creating alternative versions for each layer and turning them on and off at will. Transparent overlays were created using a mathematical formula to calculate the RGB (red, green, blue) values of the required mixture colours. The colours were mixed additively (as with light), rather than subtractively (as with pigments).

When colours are selected according to the new guidelines, the resulting displays have the following features (see [5]):

• an infilled background of medium luminance and low saturation that does not compete with foreground data;

• a transparent layering effect in the background, giving clear and unambiguous representation of overlapping areas (compare [2] and [4]);

• aircraft labels with black text and an attached colour-coded infill, thus providing greater legibility and more effective colour coding than coloured text would do;

• label infills which are clearly visible against the background whilst providing four levels of visual emphasis, each with a colour-coding facility.

Many different colour selections can be made from the palettes, but the resulting displays will always have these basic features.

For air traffic controllers, the most striking feature of the prototype displays was the use of a coloured infill behind each aircraft label. Controllers are used to text-only labels which are superimposed if there is an overlap between them. A compromise solution is shown here. Label infills are used to ensure good legibility and effective colour coding, and where labels overlap the text is superimposed as at present. The use of optimally legible fonts is crucial in minimizing the problems created by label overlap, and an electronic type design expert was called in to design appropriate fonts (not shown here).

Finally, a dynamic demonstration of the displays was developed, and groups of civil and military controllers representing different ATC applications

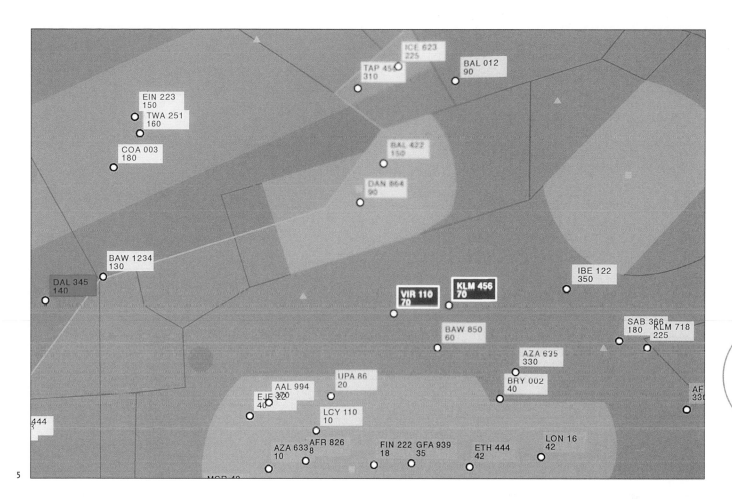

5

were invited to try out the palettes for themselves by using them to design a display. Useful comments allowed the palettes to be fine-tuned. At the NATS Air Traffic Management Development Centre at Bournemouth International Airport, there is now a simulation facility which allows the development and evaluation of ATC displays using the NATS colour palettes. This has already been used to refine specifications for civil/military displays and to evaluate display options for the New En Route Centre at Swanwick.

*Linda Reynolds*

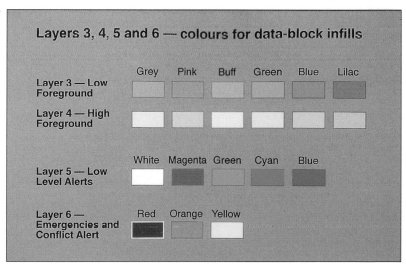

### Layers 3, 4, 5 and 6 — colours for data-block infills

|  | Grey | Pink | Buff | Green | Blue | Lilac |
|---|---|---|---|---|---|---|
| Layer 3 — Low Foreground | | | | | | |
| Layer 4 — High Foreground | | | | | | |

|  | White | Magenta | Green | Cyan | Blue |
|---|---|---|---|---|---|
| Layer 5 — Low Level Alerts | | | | | |

|  | Red | Orange | Yellow |
|---|---|---|---|
| Layer 6 — Emergencies and Conflict Alert | | | |

6

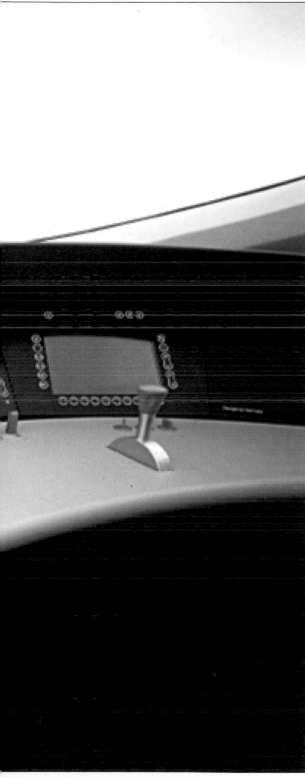

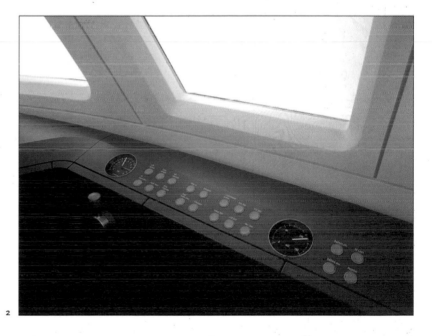

2

**1 – 2**

**InterCity Train Cockpit Design**

As part of the recent development of the InterCity and InterCity Express, high-speed trains for the Deutsche Bahn AG and other international railway companies, Siemens Design developed an entirely new modular appliance and interface concept for the train drivers' cabs in 1996. Until recently, such cabs had been organized to provide a 360-degree radius of action. With the new cab, the objective was to reduce and restructure operating elements and controls, limiting the radius of action to 180 degrees and guaranteeing an ergonomically perfect sitting and operating position. To reduce a huge amount of data to the essentials, a graphic and typographic concept was developed for the screen design, product graphics and product inscriptions, thus ensuring unified and unambiguous information. *Design: Stephan Apetauer and Frank Zebner, Siemens AG, Germany*

1

# SUI's and GUI's
## Making User Interfaces Work

*This text is from an article by Alison Black and Jacob Buur (of IDEO Product Development [for address see page 173]), edited by Rosemary Lees (Danfoss A/S, 6430 Nordborg, Denmark)*

The term 'solid user interface' (SUI) was coined in Japan to describe products with embedded microprocessors, such as video cassette recorders, photocopiers and cellular phones, and to distinguish them from the 'graphical user interfaces' (GUI's) of computer applications.

Although products with SUI's play a significant part in people's everyday lives and earn substantial revenue from sales in both industrial and consumer applications, SUI's have been a neglected area in design research. However, interest is growing.

Computing has evolved from large-scale systems to recent devices with some of the qualities of SUI's, such as Personal Digital Assistants (PDA's) like the Apple Newton. Industrial products with SUI's, once stand-alone devices used in remote workplaces, are now being integrated into organizational data-handling systems. So problems of SUI use now exist in the wider context of essential computing systems and are likely to be more visible to management. Design for usability has not kept up with the dramatic increase in functionality made possible by increasing sophistication and the miniaturization of electronic components, to the point where there is a crisis in usability which is acknowledged beyond specialist circles in the general business press. While feature promotion and price wars still dominate industrial and consumer markets for SUI products, usability is becoming a means of securing competitive advantage by manufacturers of products with SUI's.

As electronics are embedded in an increasingly wide range of products, we need to design the products themselves so that the potential the technology offers results in real benefits for users: functionality which is easy to use. This challenge brings product design into direct contact with information design, since different aspects of a SUI (its shape, configuration, graphic and sound cues, etc.) can all be harnessed to inform users about how to interact with it.

SUI's are typically limited to a restricted set of buttons and small, low-resolution displays. Limited means of interaction seem to imply difficulty for users, but these limits can be turned to users' advantage.

With the high number of functions offered by many microprocessor products, a 'one button/one function' solution is often not viable. It may take up more surface space than is available on the product (for both the buttons and their identifying labels); it is likely to be expensive to manufacture; it will at best be off-putting to users when they first confront the product; it will at worst lead to errors in use if the physical design does not allow for logical arrangement and differentiation of functions.

One of the solutions most frequently adopted to solve the problem of too many buttons is simply to hide infrequently used ones under flaps to present an apparently simple interface. Disguising interface complexity by tucking buttons away under flaps creates difficulties for users both in finding the buttons they need and in using them once they are found.

An alternative way of reducing button count is to attach several functions to each button: either by double (or triple) sets of labels with a means to

shift amongst them or, alternatively, by soft keys –
buttons tagged by variable labels which either
change automatically, according to the stage in an
interaction (the buttons are modal), or which users
can scroll through to find the function they need.
Uses need to be limited given that in many SUI's
variable information is presented on graphically
limited liquid crystal displays.

SUI's are severely restricted in their capacity for
alphabetic input. Neither of the standard options –
cursor input or modal 'international' keypads – suits
entry of more than a few characters. Solutions such
as soft keyboards on SUI displays or miniaturized
attachment keyboards have some enthusiasts, but
tend towards the 'Swiss Army knife' approach of
providing partially effective solutions to interaction
problems. There is potential for voice input,
especially as this increases users' freedom to use
products whilst on the move or in environments
where space is constrained. But voice activation
and control are fraught with difficulties for users,
and speech analysis of any level of sophistication is
likely to require processing and memory capacity
well beyond the typical SUI product.

SUI displays tend to be small, with either
segmented digits or only a few lines of dot-matrix
characters. Any attempts to use graphic displays
are likely to be constrained in size and resolution.
SUI's have additional feedback resources beyond
the display; buttons, dials and sliders can be
illuminated selectively to cue users to the correct
sequence of operation. But care is needed to
ensure that users can share attention between
input and display.

1

2

3

1 – 3

When developing a new series
of televisions, the Finnish
company Nokia Consumer
Electronics made it its goal
to improve remote control.
They commissioned the IDEO
human factors and interaction
design team to join forces
with their own team early in
the product-development
cycle. The goal was to devise
a graphical TV interface to
help viewers in different
European countries to set
up and find channels without
recourse to instruction
manuals. The designers
visited a large number of
users as well as dealers and
salespeople to identify their
needs and complaints.
This process resulted in
four scenarios, each with
its own interface concept.
These were tested on viewers
and one concept emerged
which outperformed the rest.

Products with embedded processors tend to
be more limited in power and program size
than those driven by central processing units,
so considerable ingenuity is required to make
the most of opportunities for feedback and

The chosen design concept was that of an on-screen control panel adaptable to specific size requirements and providing plain text in the language selected by the user, with a look, feel and visual connection between the keys arranged on the remote control and the on-screen representation of the interface. Users quickly learned that the keys they saw on screen were the keys active on the remote control.

4

5

6

offs between feedback and non-critical features.

Although not all products with sui's need to be battery-powered, those which have to be portable or pocketable require small batteries. Minimizing battery weight can be critical for ease of use if a product must be held single-handedly and kept balanced and stable. Compactness also often helps to sell these products and, up to a point, makes them more usable. At the same time, small batteries restrict user feedback through illuminated displays and keys and sound cues.

Despite the apparent constraints, the combined soft/hard sui interface offers opportunities for user-orientated interaction far beyond the level of many state-of-the-art products.

One button/one function solutions are highly usable provided there are not too many buttons, their functions are clearly marked or can be learned and remembered, and the buttons are differentiated adequately in position, appearance and feel. Functionality must be prioritized according to users' needs.

When there is insufficient processing capacity to drive a fully flexible display, specially designed icon characters may be used to give visual feedback, with considerably less demand on memory than full graphics.

If input components are custom-designed or dedicated to particular functions, sui's can extend beyond standard push buttons to exploit fully the hands' and fingers' capabilities. Knobs, rollers, sliders, pull rods, etc. allow precise and intuitive adjustment, often signalling a position or state more efficiently than display graphics can. Engineering to give these components tactile qualities and force feedback can augment users' sensitivity at input.

Even if cost or functionality dictate that only buttons can be used, their arrangement can be

responsiveness to user interactions. The perceived limits can force product developers into premature decisions to restrict what is displayed without weighing up the user benefits and possible trade-

planned to communicate a sequence of operation through fixed functional grouping and distinctive contouring. Combined with labelling and graphic differentiation, this can promote understanding of use in a more effective way than with flexible GUI displays.

A new approach, which could simplify modal interaction, is to change buttons, rather than labels, according to interaction mode. With a flexible casing material, buttons required at any point of interaction can be shaped and raised from the surface when needed by means of active, computer-controlled elements underneath and then removed from the perceptible interface when they are not required.

SUI's give freedom to shape the physical form of the interface to fit users' hands and body postures. This opportunity is being exploited for hand-held measuring equipment, ticketing devices, etc. They also provide opportunities to build product identity by exploiting three-dimensional, visual and sound qualities. Carried across a range of products, SUI's can literally have an identifiable 'feel' which communicates product features and functionality very directly to new users.

Unfortunately, software engineers are not automatically good designers of interfaces for people who do not share their specialist experience of a product. Organizations developing SUI products need to research their users' needs to draw on a wider range of user experience than their own engineers can provide. SUI's, however, are often incidental tools for mobile work (such as industrial control devices) or leisure activities (electronic games) where user interactions cannot be replicated well outside the real use environment. Designers need to make sure they engage with end users in their own environments (albeit sometimes inhospitable or private ones) in order to understand user requirements from the earliest stages of product development.

Similarly, as designers develop prototypes they must test them in the environment in which the products will be used. New methods are required to ensure a good fit between innovative products and their proposed environments. An example is 'Informance', where designers act out future user scenarios in realistic settings in order to understand and communicate the impact of new designs. SUI's can be partially represented on touch screens, but at some point prototypes representing the dimensions and weight of the product must be made because the real arrangement of the components influences the smoothness of user interactions. Three dimensional modelling of products is more expensive and less flexible than screen-based modelling, so economizing by producing a series of approximations to the finished product is generally accepted.

Solid user interfaces have informative qualities and offer potential for interactions which – at least for some users, tasks and environments – are superior to GUI technology. Research is necessary to establish the best organizational structures, development tools and techniques to bring about increased SUI usability. Manufacturers must become more orientated to end users than at present, and usability design needs to be involved early on in the product-development process and supported by prototyping tools and testing which allows close replication of real use conditions. The tools must help to bridge hardware and software, combining the skills of scientists, industrial designers, graphic and information designers and hardware and software engineers to deliver user-centred solutions.       *Rosemary Lees (ed.)*

# 4  Interacting with the Screen

Kiosk Systems • Multimedia CD-ROM's • Web Sites

Prior to the introduction of computers, there were very few examples of interactivity as the term is used in today's computer age. One of these – still of interest because of its portability, low cost and effectiveness in dealing with a limited range of information – is the printed 'information wheel'. In a similar format, the 'slide-rule' type of presentation also continues to have uses. These two formats have been employed for storing miniature 'programs' on such topics as weather forecasting, currency conversion, local and national radio frequencies and, in a more specialized way, the symptoms of drug abuse (a tool produced for the police). The range of subject-matter is only limited by the capacity of the format (anything between a diameter of sixty and three hundred millimetres). The wheel version is activated by revolving one of the discs to indicate the question, the 'answers' to which are

shown in the pre-cut 'windows' of the outer disc.

Interaction with a computer is now invariably achieved by means of a standard 'qwerty' keyboard. As is well documented, this keyboard layout was developed for early mechanical typewriters to slow down their operators so as to avoid jamming the mechanical links between the keys and the letter dies. This standard keyboard is so firmly imbedded in our culture that it is deemed impossible to change it for a system which would work more quickly and efficiently on a computer.

At least one serious attempt has been made to update the 'qwerty' layout, however. The Microwriting system [1] developed in the early 1970s replaces the fifty 'qwerty' keys with just five keys set out to mimic the natural position of the fingertips, one for each finger of the right hand (the system assumes a right-handed user). A sixth key is used for commands. The fingers remain fixed

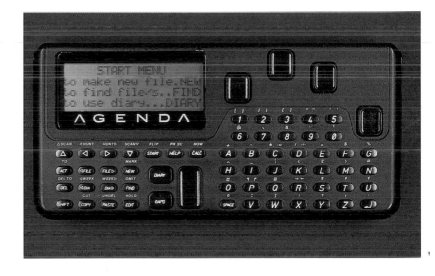

above this set of keys, and by pressing different paired combinations, something like sixty-four characters can be selected. The system has recently been adapted to replace a standard personal-computer keyboard and has a small, dedicated band of users. Its claimed advantages include speed of learning, the achievement of higher keyboard speeds and complete portability.

Human input into computer programs has evolved over a period of time from the earliest machines which required input via switches or punched cards to the screen input of alphanumeric codes and, more recently, to the selecting of appropriate visual icons. During the early stages, when most computer users still required a knowledge of programming in order to get the most from their systems, it was natural to conduct the input in a coded language, but as computers became more widespread and programs were

aimed at more specific office routines such as letter writing and financial accounting, it became increasingly wearisome to have to remember meaningless strings of keyboard characters.

Apple were one of the first to introduce graphic icons to the screen. These symbols were chosen to represent most of the functions of a program and to mimic as closely as possible objects found in the average business environment so that even an untrained operator could visualize the program's operation. The filing-cabinet icon stood for the hard disc, the file stood for the letter or

## Microwriting

Microwriting, a system of chord keying, is based on a set of mnemonics developed by Cy Endfield and Chris Rainey in the 1970s. The system was incorporated into the Microwriter hand-held word processor and, subsequently, the Microwriter AgendA personal organizer, shown here. These are no longer available, but Microwriting lives on in the form of a PC keyboard called CyKey, named after Endfield.

2

**Corporate Law Presentation**

This multimedia program demonstrates how complex legal issues can be presented in a non-linear form, with the layered integration of text, video footage [3] and diagrams [4, 6]. A main tool bar [2] provides visual metaphors for each function and Hypertext links are indicated in colour.
*Design: Dynamic Diagrams, U.S.A*

document holder and the waste bin stood for deleting documents from the memory. The two input systems are still with us, but it seems that the more intuitive icon is winning the day.

In the early days, it was realized that the digital basis of computing provided the ideal medium for linking together an unlimited number of inputs. Initially, in the text realm, users were able to select personal routes through a list of alternatives on offer. Then hypertext was developed.

Closely linked with the name of counter-culture guru Ted Nelson, who proposed the name of Xanadu for it in 1967, hypertext referred to a program which enabled a given text to be linked to any number of subtexts (similar to a collection of information on file cards) and which also enabled its user to select a pathway through them. The user could start or exit at any point or return to the beginning, and, if the texts were carefully constructed, could create a seamless, personalized statement based on them. This was the ideal format for a whole range of applications based on the search/browse mode of use such as encyclopaedias and reference books. Conceptually, it was but a small step to include not only linking text references but imagery, animation, sound and video, thus creating the basis of present-day multimedia programs [2–6]. One of the forces contributing to the rapid development of the necessary technology was the demands made by the programmers and users of electronic games, particularly in their complex arcade versions.

Multimedia applications are usually accessed by clicking on to icons on a screen by means of a

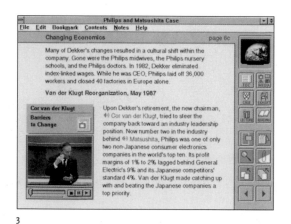

3

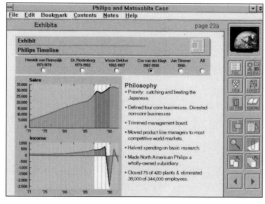

4

5

6

mouse [7–8]. A touch-screen – whereby a grid of touch-sensitive areas, sometimes labelled graphically, is superimposed on a standard screen – can be made to activate a series of choices or updates of information and has a number of advantages over the use of a mouse in certain situations. For people not familiar with computers, a touch-screen has a more intuitive feel, but it can present design problems, as the touch-sensitive areas have to be of a certain minimum size to prevent the user accidently pressing the wrong command button.

In the area of public interactivity, the use of multimedia has proven to be extremely successful for information points or 'kiosks' used by visitors to museums, public parks and exhibitions, where it is possible to provide an enormous range of related information at the beginning or indeed at any stage of their progress through an event. Touch-screens have an advantage in situations in which the user is likely to access the program while standing (which precludes the use of a mouse) and in which many visitors might be reluctant to take the time to sit down in front of a computer screen. One disadvantage of the kiosk type of information point is that only a few people at a time can view a single screen; this can be problematic if visitors are likely to arrive in large batches on, say, coaches or trains. In such situations, a printed guide can still be the best solution, but there are alternatives such as a collection of monitors raised above normal eye-level or large, projection-type TV screens. Multimedia presentations can also make another valuable contribution in that they can present text and audio information in a number of selected languages.

It may be too early to say what the ideal way might be to present information to the public: an actual guide, multimedia on screen, hand-held

audio players or printed matter. But there can be no doubt that digital technology in both its present and possible future forms will provide a powerful addition to conventional methods of communicating information to large audiences.

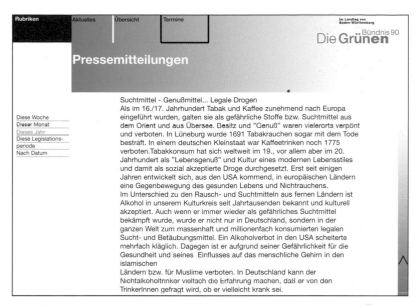

7

8

### German Green Party Web Site

This web site represents an integrated component of the corporate identity which was developed during 1997 for the Green Party in the Baden Württemburg state parliament.
*Design: Büro für Gestaltung, Miedander, Burke, Hoffmann, Germany*

**1 – 2**
**Kaufhof Galleria Multimedia Kiosk**

Inspiration for this interface design came from the interior design of Kaufhof's new media and technology departments. The grid system allows future kiosk systems to be adjusted to their respective environments within this large German department store chain by using other colours, textures and typefaces whilst retaining a consistent look and interface. This is important to Kaufhof shoppers, who will be seeing these systems in various other departments in the future.

1

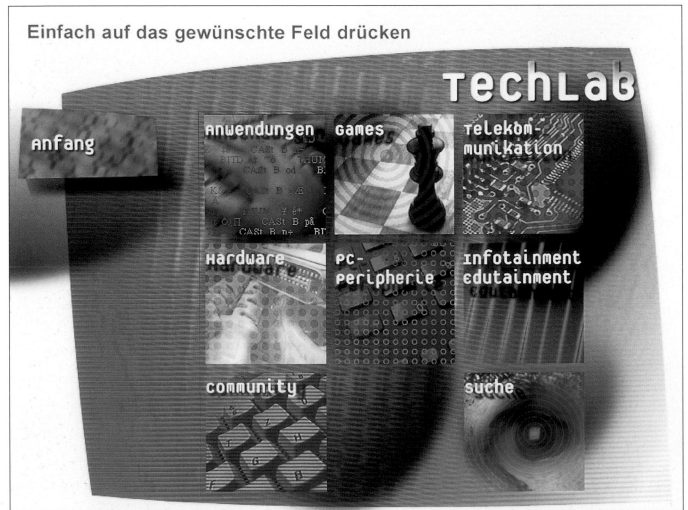

2

Einfach auf das gewünschte Feld drücken

3

3 – 7
**Kaufhof Galleria Multimedia Kiosk**

This series of screens illustrates the interface design for the kiosk, an interactive system with databanks. The first of these touch-screen applications, 'Touch the Music', provides rapid access to music and video clips. Search engines offer users many ways of finding a particular piece. The databanks are continually being updated, and shoppers can even take a CD off the rack, scan its bar code into the system and listen to clips of the tracks on it.
*Marketing concept and general contractor: mmk Multimedia Kommunikations AG, Germany; visual concept and screen production: scopo, Switzerland*

Text eintippen, starten mit "Suche", mit "ok" anzeigen lassen

4

Der Touch the Music Special Service

5

Auswählen, auf das Cover drücken, Musik hören

6

Mit Stop zurück zur vorhergehenden Seite

7

# A National Park Multimedia Program

## Informing Visitors in Four Languages

The Swiss National Park in Zerneg, Graubünden, is one of the largest nature reserves in Switzerland and, because of its great scenic beauty, is extremely popular with walkers and naturalists. This interactive information system was initiated by Hans Kren, then a student in his final semester in the department of visual communication at the School of Design in Basel. Kren proposed as a post-graduate project the theme of 'the computer as an information source in the public sector'. A prototype was produced to test the possibility of using what was then the relatively new medium of multimedia and to find out what advantages it could offer over traditional media. There were many aspects of the project that had to be explored before it could go ahead; these included considerations as to the nature of the interface, the accessibility of the screen to groups of people rather than individuals, the means of navigating through the system, and the balance of text-based information versus still and moving imagery.

Contact was made with the National Park officials, the Geographic Institute of Zürich University and experts on conservation and wildlife. The final outcome after many meetings was a decision by the National Park to give the go-ahead for the designer to produce a multimedia system to run alongside its existing visitor centres. A prototype was produced in 1994 which later came to be known as DIBIS (Digital Visitor's Information System). It was decided that the new information points should be set up at each of the Park's entrances and that one of their main functions would be to relieve staff from having to answer the same visitors' questions over and over again. The target audience was younger visitors familiar with the technology, but was not meant to exclude other age groups. The interactive system had to be multilingual. (At present, it is available in four languages.) It was agreed that the new information points would not take the place of existing facilities such as slide shows, talks, a bookshop and an information desk, but would augment them to allow visitors to explore those areas of particular interest to them and to provide unrivalled factual information which would be updated as appropriate. Visitors could explore topographical information, transport connections and a range of wildlife and plants and could work out their own special-interest nature trails.

The main problem associated with monitor screens used in public places is the number of

1

The two sections of the screen design can be seen clearly: the menu (left) and orientation and thematic section (right).

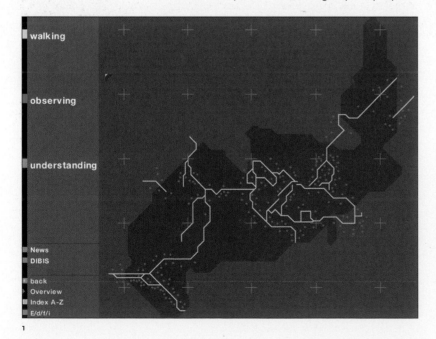

1

reflections they pick up from their surroundings. These can be overcome by careful positioning of the monitor with regard to natural and artificial light sources, but the effect can also be reduced by avoiding large areas of dark screen content whenever possible. As with many screen-based projects, one of the first problems to arise was the quality and legibility of type matter when viewed on the screen, a concern of some importance as it was planned that the screen should be watchable by groups of people rather than single viewers.

Working with a screen resolution of only seventy-two dots per inch produced less than perfect legibility even in relatively large type sizes. The problem was eventually solved by using anti-aliasing techniques which soften the jagged outlines of the letter forms by creating what is effectively a slightly out-of-focus image. One of the side-effects of this technique is that the type matter requires a little more spacing between the individual letters which make up a word; this can also pose legibility problems. A further constraint was that the colour range was limited to 256 colours, which meant that a careful selection had to be made to accommodate different backgrounds, a range of maps and the colour coding of the content sections.

The screen layout is divided vertically into a navigation panel on the left and an image area on the right of almost square format. The only exception is the use of a wide-screen format which occupies the entire screen width for certain pictorial and landscape sequences. The content of the program is divided into three colour-coded areas

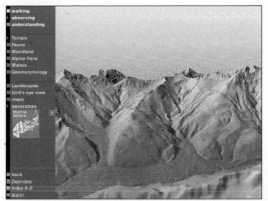

2

2 – 3

A large component of the interactive display is visualized by means of relief maps (3-D models) from which the topology of the Park is easily understood. [3] compares the relative heights of various mountains in the Park, with maps provided by Zürich's Geographical Institute.

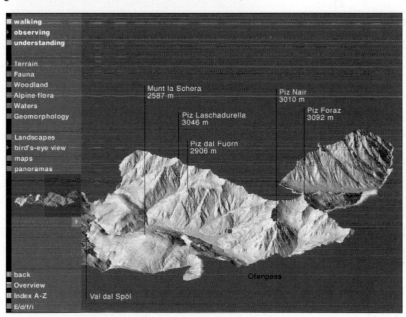

3

which can broadly be described as 'walks', 'observation' and 'understanding'. Walks include nature trails as well as information on transport connections; observation includes information on the birds, wildlife, plants and trees; understanding includes a large database of information about the historical, scientific

**4**

Walks are a major aspect of the Zerneg National Park. This screen shows one layer of the program's contents as a series of walks. On the left-hand side of the screen is the navigation panel, which orientates the user.

**5**

Another layout of the map reveals the Park's highest peaks, illustrated by dots, where the relationship and distance between them can be seen in plan.

**6**

As there are visitors of different ages and fitness levels, a chart illustrates the severity of the walks' gradients, which is coded to tie into the system of numbers on the walks map [4].

**7**

A third level of the maps indicates bus routes and times. The integration of the bus map with walking routes allows visitors to plan one-way journeys.

and ecological aspects of the National Park.

Navigation through the system is controlled from the left-hand panel, enabling the viewer to click onto the language required and then to engage with a particular theme, call up a contents list or alphabetical index, and return to the main screen. To get deeper into the content, buttons are provided, and in some cases areas on the right of the screen can be activated. When the cursor moves over one of these sensitized areas, it is illuminated and its point starts to blink, indicating that further information is available.

Maps play an important role in the program, enabling visitors to view the local terrain by means of a series of highly detailed relief diagrams prepared by the Geographic Institute as well

as maps detailing local walks, nature trails and transport connections within the region. The complexity and severity of the tourist trails are presented through various graphic and tabular treatments for different age groups and fitness levels. A special feature of some of the terrain maps is that it is possible to view them with the shadows cast by the sun in the correct position according to the time of day, an important consideration when planning a route along a valley. The history and scientific aspects of the National Park are also included in the program, augmented with video sequences supplied by Swiss Television. The program has a section on the ecological concerns connected with the Park such as problems of industrial encroachment, pollution, hydroelectric power and the sheer numbers of

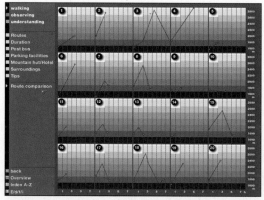

4

6

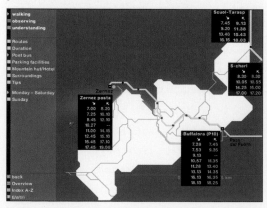

5

7

visitors. In total, there are some 220 screen
'pages'. These would take at least an hour to view
in sequence, but of course most viewers only
select material of immediate interest to them.
Sound is used sparingly so as not to distract
from the ambient sounds of the surroundings
and is confined to the video sequences and a
few bird songs.

A touch screen was originally considered, but
there were a number of arguments against its use
in this context. A touch screen's 'sensitive' areas
have to be relatively large and set in a standard
matrix which limits their flexibility in the screen
layout; also, there is a loss of feedback due to lack
of a 'blinking' function and the eventual smearing
of the glass screen with repeated use.

So that as many people as possible can view the
screen, the user is seated at a low table with the
monitor installed higher up. This way about ten
people can comfortably view the screen at any one
time. The user operates the system with an
integrated track ball. Consideration was given to
providing a means of printing out from the screen,
but there were financial limitations, especially
for colour printing, and problems of having to
service the printer with paper and toner as well
as considerations of possible vandalism. It was
also felt that printed output might conflict with
existing printed matter available at the general
information desk.

After several years of intensive use, this
interactive system is well tested. Staff at the centres
and those in contact with walkers out on the trails
feel that visitors are much better informed on all
aspects of the Park and its ecosystem than before.
The system is now a major component in informing
visitors and can be in almost continuous use over
the course of a busy day.                    *Hans Kren*

8

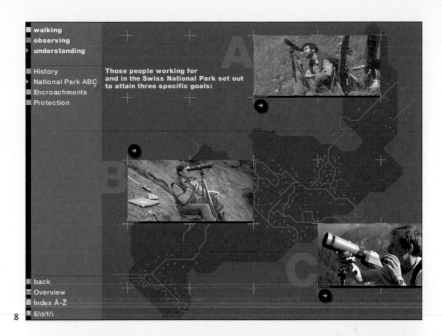

9

**8**

The work of scientists in the
areas of geology, surveying
and ornithology is explored in
a scientific section which
includes video footage.

**9**

Another section presents the
ecology and the way in which
the Zerneg National Park
deals with the encroachment
of industrialization and the
protection of species.

1

2

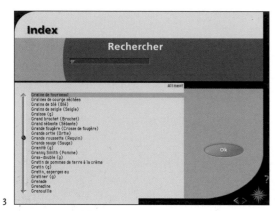

3

4

**1 – 8**

**Multimedia Cookbook**

This interactive cookbook on CD-ROM contains a whole spectrum of dishes and combinations. The screen design utilizes the now almost universal methods of scrolling and key words which lead the user to additional information by means of 'pop-ups' when they are activated by clicking with a mouse. Navigation is done through buttons and pictograms.

*Design: QA International, Canada*

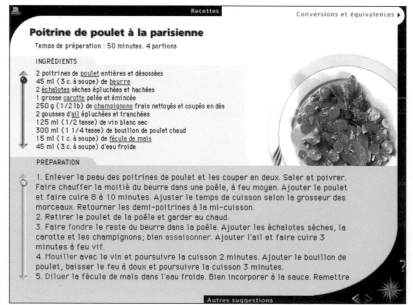

5

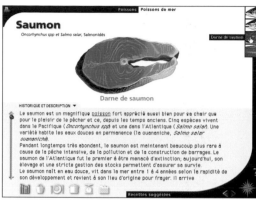

## Saumon

*Oncorhynchus spp et Salmo salar*, Salmonidés

Darne de saumon

**HISTORIQUE ET DESCRIPTION** ▾

Le saumon est un magnifique poisson fort apprécié aussi bien pour sa chair que pour le plaisir de le pêcher et ce, depuis les temps anciens. Cinq espèces vivent dans le Pacifique (*Oncorhynchus spp*) et une dans l'Atlantique (*Salmo salar*). Une variété habite les eaux douces en permanence (la ouananiche, *Salmo salar ouananiche*).

Pendant longtemps très abondant, le saumon est maintenant beaucoup plus rare à cause de la pêche intensive, de la pollution et de la construction de barrages. Le saumon de l'Atlantique fut le premier à être menacé d'extinction; aujourd'hui, son élevage et une stricte gestion des stocks permettent d'assurer sa survie.

Le saumon naît en eau douce, vit dans la mer entre 1 à 4 années selon la rapidité de son développement et revient à son lieu d'origine pour frayer. Il arrive

Recettes suggérées

6

Poissons **Poissons de mer**

## Saumon

*Oncorhynchus spp et Salmo salar*, Salmonidés

Filefer un poisson rond

**HISTORIQUE ET DESCRIPTION** ▾

Le saumon est un magnifique poisson fort apprécié aussi bien pour sa chair que pour le plaisir de le pêcher et ce, depuis les temps anciens. Cinq espèces vivent dans le Pacifique (*Oncorhynchus spp*) et une dans l'Atlantique (*Salmo salar*). Une variété habite les eaux douces en permanence (la ouananiche, *Salmo salar ouananiche*).

Pendant longtemps très abondant, le saumon est maintenant beaucoup plus rare à cause de la pêche intensive, de la pollution et de la construction de barrages. Le saumon de l'Atlantique fut le premier à être menacé d'extinction; aujourd'hui, son élevage et une stricte gestion des stocks permettent d'assurer sa survie.

Le saumon naît en eau douce, vit dans la mer entre 1 à 4 années selon la rapidité de son développement et revient à son lieu d'origine pour frayer. Il arrive

Recettes suggérées

7

# Saumon

*Oncorhynchus spp et Salmo salar*, Salmonidés

Saumon de l'Atlantique

**UTILISATION**

La chair du côté de la tête est plus délicate que celle près de la queue. Le saumon fumé est souvent accompagné de câpres et d'oignons doux émincés. On l'utilise pour donner une touche spéciale aux aliments, te[...]des, les omelettes, les pâtes alimentaires, les mou[...]de masquer sa saveur.

Le saumon en conserve est cuit et mis en b[...]es et ses vertèbres sont souvent présentes. On peut f[...]elles sont très friables et constituent une intéressant[...]umon en conserve a une utilisation très variée. On le[...]sandwichs, les salades, les sauces, les omelettes et le[...]mousse, en soufflé, en pâté et en crêpes. Il est aussi pr[...], utilisé

Recettes suggérées

Courgettes farcies au saumon
Darnes de saumon au basilic
Darnes de saumon pochées au...
Fettucine au saumon fumé et...
Rigatoni au saumon en sauce...
Salade au saumon
Salade d'avocats, de pample...
Salade de moules au vinaigr...
Saumon en papillote
Saumon fumé sur Pumpernickel
Sushis
Tomates farcies au saumon fumé

8

## 1 – 6

**Multimedia Encyclopaedia**

Illustrated here is a comprehensive visual encyclopaedia published on CD-ROM. It utilizes a variety of visual models from drawings to photographic images. A general button navigation system is situated along the bottom of the screen with an additional area allocated at the top left for specific use — to change the orientation of diagrams, for example.
*Design: QA International, Canada*

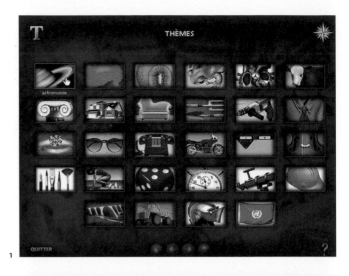

1

2

3

4

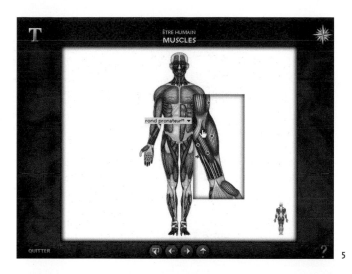

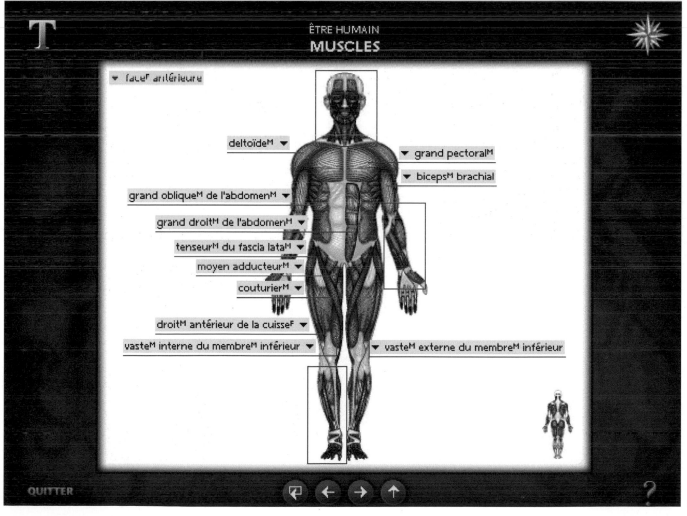

▼ face[F] antérieure

deltoïde[M] ▼

▼ grand pectoral[M]

▼ biceps[M] brachial

grand oblique[M] de l'abdomen[M] ▼

grand droit[M] de l'abdomen[M] ▼

tenseur[M] du fascia lata[M] ▼

moyen adducteur[M] ▼

couturier[M] ▼

droit[M] antérieur de la cuisse[F] ▼

vaste[M] interne du membre[M] inférieur ▼

▼ vaste[M] externe du membre[M] inférieur

QUITTER

**Geva Institute Web Site**

It is unusual for a market research company to adopt such a strong visual concept as was developed for this corporate identity. It was clear from the outset of the project that the electronic medium was going to play an important role in the communication process. Another important issue was that information would have to be easy to update by in-house personnel. The design of the web site uses a restricted colour selection of red, black and white with the occasional key colour image.

**3 – 5**

**Geva Institute Web Site**

These screen designs used databanks that were compiled from research questionnaires. The statistics were resourced from employees of large companies, collated and put into a visual model using a percentage scale.

*Design: Kognito, Germany*

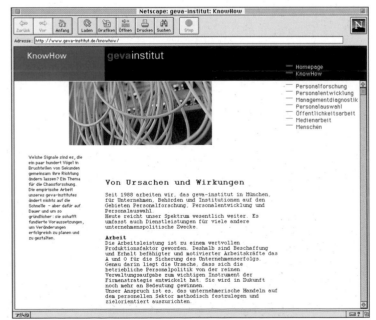

**gevaVIZ**

Dargestellten Bereich löschen
Refer.
Refer.Gesch5.
Refer.Gesch5.Abtei5.
Refer.Gesch5.Abtei5.Arbei8.

Bereich übernehmen
Referenzunternehmen
Geschäftsbereich 5
Abteilung 5
Arbeitsgruppe 8

| ... weitere Themen | Grafik | Tabelle | Prozent | Mittelwert | Tendenz | Ausgewählten Bereich löschen |
|---|---|---|---|---|---|---|
| Thema Nr. 1 Hg345678901234567890123345 | 10% | 91% | 30% | | 71% | |
| Thema Nr. 2 Hg345678901234567890123345 | 15% | 93% | 29% | | 68% | |
| Thema Nr. 3 Hg345678901234567890123345 | 9% | 98% | 29% | | 72% | |
| Thema Nr. 4 Hg345678901234567890123345 | 16% | 91% | 26% | | 74% | |
| Thema Nr. 5 Hg345678901234567890123345 | 18% | 96% | 27% | | 72% | |
| Thema Nr. 6 Hg345678901234567890123345 | 14% | 97% | 26% | | 72% | |
| Thema Nr. 7 Hg345678901234567890123345 | 10% | 93% | 27% | | 77% | |
| Thema Nr. 8 Hg345678901234567890123345 | 18% | 91% | 25% | | 77% | |
| Thema Nr. 9 Hg345678901234567890123345 | 16% | 89% | 26% | | 68% | |
| Thema Nr. 10 Hg345678901234567890123345 | 11% | 97% | 27% | | 70% | |

3

**gevaVIZ**

Dargestellten Bereich löschen
Refer.
Refer.Gesch5.
Refer.Gesch5.Abtei5.
Refer.Gesch5.Abtei5.Arbei8.

Bereich übernehmen
Referenzunternehmen
Geschäftsbereich 5
Abteilung 5
Arbeitsgruppe 8

| ... weitere Themen | Grafik | Tabelle | Prozent | Mittelwert | Tendenz | Ausgewählten Bereich löschen |
|---|---|---|---|---|---|---|
| Thema Nr. 1 Hg345678901234567890123345 | 20 | 40 | 60 | 80 | 100 | |
| Thema Nr. 2 Hg345678901234567890123345 | | | | | | |
| Thema Nr. 3 Hg345678901234567890123345 | | | | | | |
| Thema Nr. 4 Hg345678901234567890123345 | | | | | | |
| Thema Nr. 5 Hg345678901234567890123345 | | | | | | |
| Thema Nr. 6 Hg345678901234567890123345 | | | | | | |
| Thema Nr. 7 Hg345678901234567890123345 | | | | | | |
| Thema Nr. 8 Hg345678901234567890123345 | | | | | | |
| Thema Nr. 9 Hg345678901234567890123345 | | | | | | |
| Thema Nr. 10 Hg345678901234567890123345 | | | | | | |

4

# gevaVIZ

| Ausgewählte Themen löschen | Dargestellten Bereich löschen | Bereich übernehmen |
|---|---|---|
| Thema Nr. 11 Hg345678901234567890123345 | Refer. Refer.Gesch5. Refer.Gesch5.Abtei5. Refer.Gesch5.Abtei5.Arbei8. | Referenzunternehmen Geschäftsbereich 5 Abteilung 5 Arbeitsgruppe 8 |

| ... vorherige Themen | Grafik | Tabelle | Prozent | Mittelwert | Tendenz | Ausgewählten Bereich löschen |
|---|---|---|---|---|---|---|
| | 20 | 40 | 60 | 80 | 100 | |
| Frage 11 zu Thema 11 Hg345678901234567890123345 | | | | | | |
| Frage 12 zu Thema 11 Hg345678901234567890123345 | | | | | | |
| Frage 13 zu Thema 11 Hg345678901234567890123345 | | | | | | |
| Frage 14 zu Thema 11 Hg345678901234567890123345 | | | | | | |
| Frage 15 zu Thema 11 Hg345678901234567890123345 | | | | | | |
| Frage 16 zu Thema 11 Hg345678901234567890123345 | | | | | | |
| Frage 17 zu Thema 11 Hg345678901234567890123345 | | | | | | |
| Frage 18 zu Thema 11 Hg345678901234567890123345 | | | | | | |
| Frage 19 zu Thema 11 Hg345678901234567890123345 | | | | | | |
| Frage 20 zu Thema 11 Hg345678901234567890123345 | | | | | | |

5

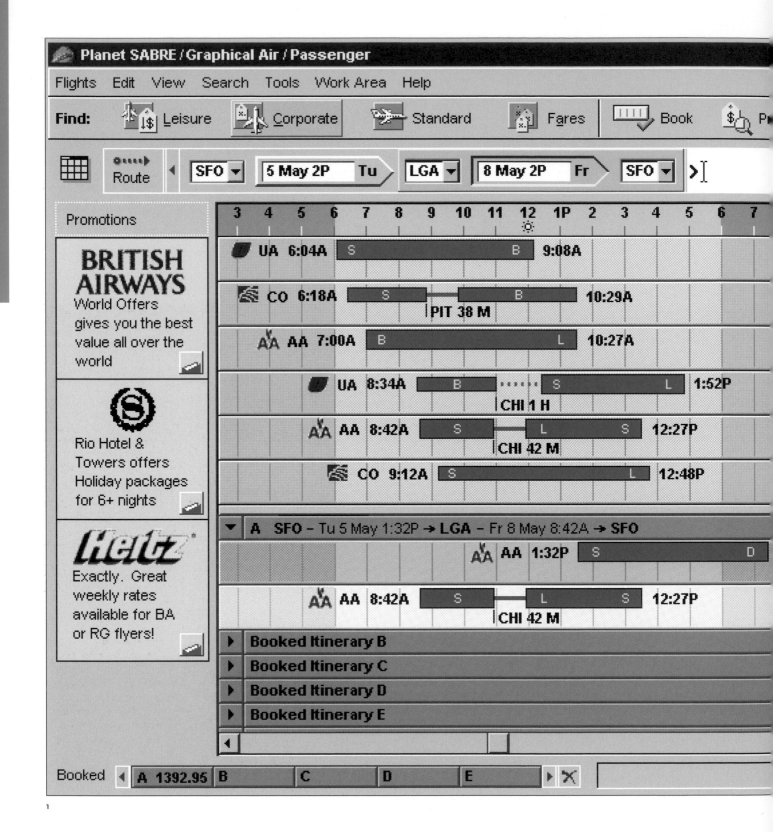

1

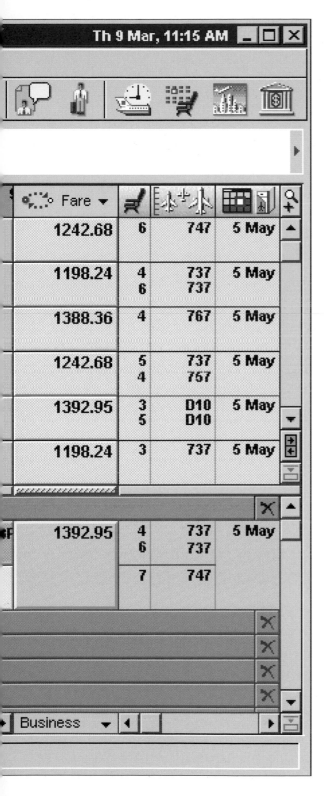

**1**

**Planet SABRE 2.0 Graphical Air Booking System**

In 1995–97, the office of Aaron Marcus and Associates, Inc. designed an innovative user interface for one of the world's largest private on-line information systems, Planet SABRE. This system is used by thirty-seven per cent of travel agents world-wide. So that the SABRE 'Travel Information Network' would continue to lead the market in technical reliability and ease of use, its complex command-line user interface for booking air travel was completely redesigned. The project began by researching how travel agents used SABRE and how they worked with their customers to help them reach purchasing decisions. Particular problems with Graphical Air, as the new system was called, were the integration of airline advertising messages with generic product offers [1] and interactive operators. The system required universally recognized metaphors, formats and signs suitable for different languages and cultures. Also, different travel patterns and booking practices had to be accommodated.
*Design principal: Aaron Marcus and Associates, Inc., U.S.A.*

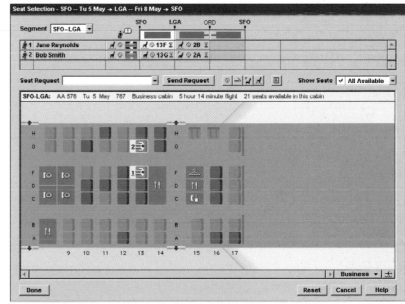

**2**

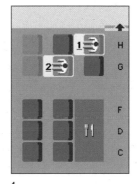

**3**

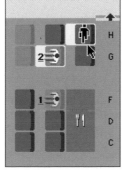

**4**

**2 – 4**
**Planet SABRE 2.0 Graphical Air Booking System**

Specialized visualization and interaction techniques [2–4] of the finished product include graphic timelines which allow quicker readings of flight characteristics when compared with more traditional alphanumeric depictions.

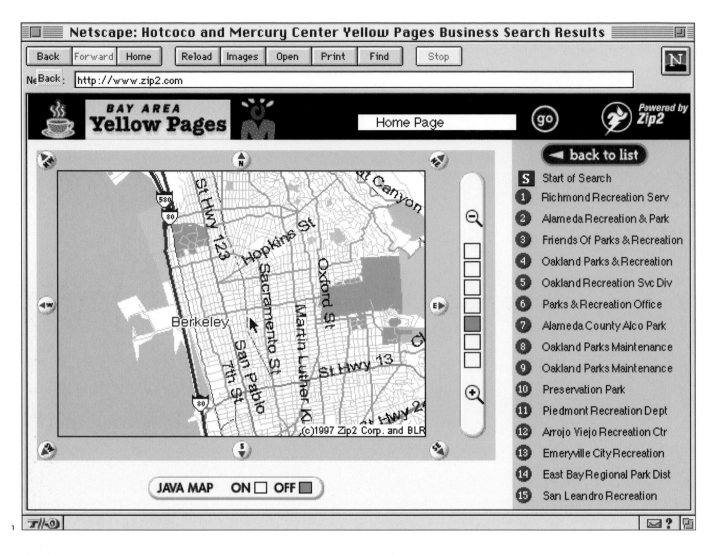

1

2

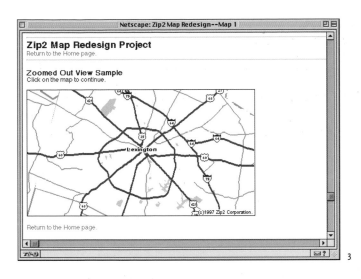

**Netscape: Zip2 Map Redesign--Map 1**

**Zip2 Map Redesign Project**
Return to the Home page.

**Zoomed Out View Sample**
Click on the map to continue.

Return to the Home page.

3

Zip2 is a leading provider of web-site-based information for the American *Yellow Pages*, a business directory of companies and their products organized alphabetically by business category. The two main areas in which the design consultants were involved were the use of colour and the design of the maps. The latter, while based on familiar traditional models, were optimized for use on screen. Careful attention was paid to the colour range to enable the web site to be used by individuals with colour-deficient eyesight.
*Design: Aaron Marcus and Associates, Inc.,* U.S.A.

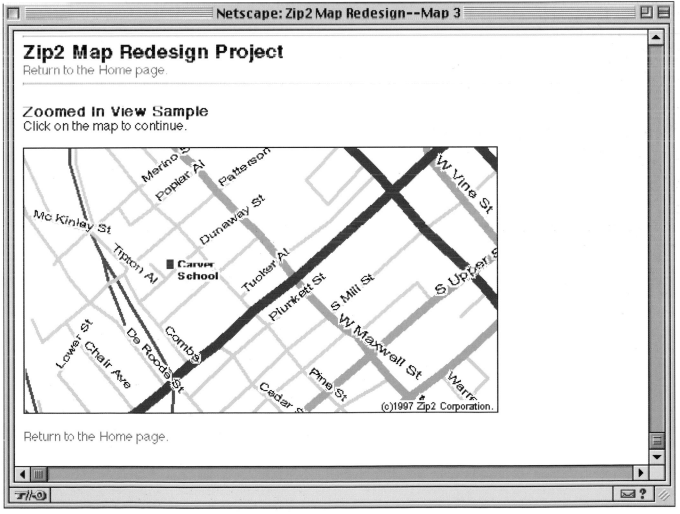

**Netscape: Zip2 Map Redesign--Map 3**

# Zip2 Map Redesign Project
Return to the Home page.

## Zoomed In View Sample
Click on the map to continue.

Return to the Home page.

4

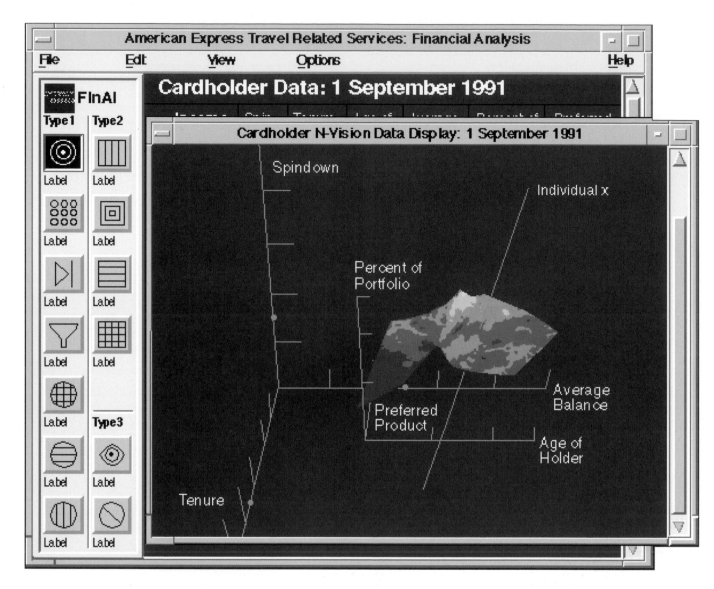

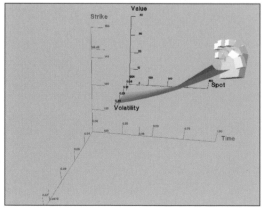

**1 – 4**

**American Express Web Site Design**

American Express is a major international travel-related company which deals in particular with credit cards and travellers cheques. The objectives of this prototype model for future applications was to improve the ability of financial analysts to view credit-card holders' records and made recommendations regarding their current and future status. The design consultants researched various multidimensional statistical methods before settling on two basic ones, Feiner and Besher's 'N Vision' and Iselberg's parallel co-ordinates system. *Design: Aaron Marcus and Associates, Inc., U.S.A.*

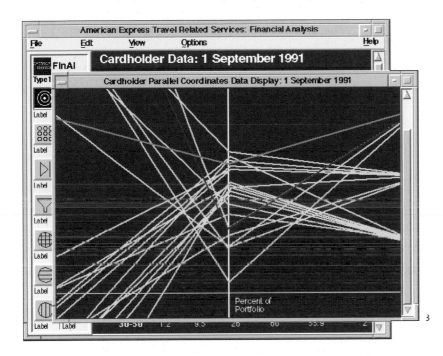

3

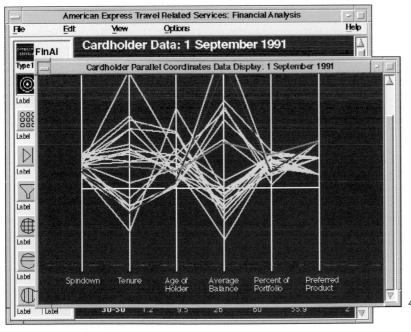

4

# Reuters Web
## Designing an On-line Direct Marketing Service

Reuters is the world's leading news and financial information company, supplying information for professionals who use it to help them in their businesses. In 1996, the company launched the 3000 series of products, giving customers access to a huge new database of historical information. This database used the latest massive parallel-processing techniques to achieve a rapid search of vast quantities of information.

Reuters Web is offered in conjunction with the 3000 service, a so-called Extranet using the same technology as the public Internet. As an Extranet, it is restricted to Reuters customers and is therefore more secure and reliable than the Internet. Reuters wanted to take advantage of the Web's unique strengths in supporting direct marketing and promotion efforts, servicing their 3000 customers and building better business relationships one customer at a time.

The aim of the service was to host non-business/leisure information, providing a showcase of special offers and rewards. By building a web site, Reuters could capture professional and personal information through on-line registration forms and subscriber transactions as direct data for future strategic marketing campaigns.

The Reuters City Service was launched as part of a strategic pilot scheme in Belgium and the Netherlands. We proposed to design a prototype which fulfilled two clear functions: to create an aspirational model of the service that could be used as a bench-mark for the development of the pilot scheme, and to provide Reuters with a platform for demonstrating the service to a select group of global brands in their efforts to attract participants who could provide a regular supply of special offers as incentives for client feedback.

One of the main requirements of the design was to support a mechanism which allowed Reuters to create and target messages to registered customers as easy-access links to offers and promotions in which they had expressed interest and which had been updated since their last visit to the web site. To achieve this, customer profiles had to be put into a database and made accessible through a set of administration tools enabling dedicated staff to perform one-to-one marketing and promote special offers to the right segments of the client base.

The original specification required a set of editorial containers that held categories of information under a list of static service titles. To access this information, customers would have needed to select a container in order to view its content. We rejected this structure as problematic because it would have committed Reuters to supplying a continuous stream of content to fill each container on a regular basis. A category for wine editorial, for example, only allowed for wine-related content. We wanted to develop a set of containers based on themes which could be filled with a diverse mix of content as it was made available. By allowing these containers to be large or small, we could provide as little or as much content as was available. We were adapting publishing conventions established in the world of print to the latest web technology capabilities.

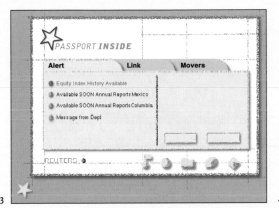

1

2

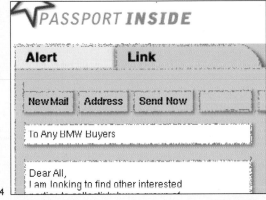

3

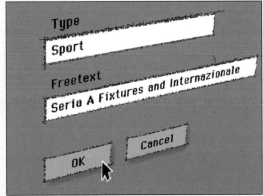

4

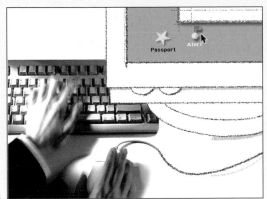

5

6

The process by which
on-screen sketches and
storyboards were developed
in the early stages of
the design process.
Each storyboard depicted a
scenario which described
the sequence of tasks a user
could perform when using
the service. The storyboards
helped the designers to
communicate, consider and
re-evaluate some of the more
abstract concepts which
had been outlined in the
project requirements.

Our project team of necessity reflected the
interdisciplinary concerns of interactive design,
since the service we offer considers the design of
effective interactions between people and machines
and amongst people using machines. However, as
the group was purposely small, each member was
used to playing various roles and led or supported
team effort depending on the nature of the work
and needs of the project.

We started by considering what we wanted a
typical customer to experience when using this
service. Together with Reuters, we wrote a number
of detailed scenarios which described design ideas
and themes as fictional stories set in the context of

7

7 – 10

These images show how the
user interface was designed to
a grid structure, according to
the cycle of daily, weekly and
monthly content [**9, 10**], which
divides the screen into units
of editorial containers.

8

realistic situations. Each scenario was used as a framework in which to consider the different navigational paths, information flow and service structures which together would determine the kind of experience a customer might have. These ideas evolved into a set of preliminary story-boards that depicted the sequence of tasks performed by a customer and communicated some of the key concepts behind the design.

From these initial designs, we developed a model of the service in the form of an on-line prototype which demonstrated the timing, function and behaviour of the design. Developing the prototype also allowed us to tackle a number of important issues concerning the identity of the service, as well as wider issues concerning the look and feel of the web site.

It was very important for us to keep the development of the design in line with the aims and objectives of the database software developers. Once created, the prototype served as a forum to review and discuss the progress of the design and helped to co-ordinate the development and implementation of the pilot. Integrating the design and development process ensured that any discrepancies between the prototype and the pilot based on technical constraints became apparent within the design development process. The flexibility of the prototype allowed us to react to these issues and modify the design accordingly. World brands were asked to participate in the service by providing a mixture of special offers as a way of creating incentives for client feedback in direct marketing efforts. Demonstrating the prototype to third parties helped to communicate how they could be involved in making the service a reality.                    *Rodney Edwards*

9

10

# 5 Exploring the 3-D Interface

Virtual Space • Assembly Manuals • Orientation Diagrams • Exploded Diagrams • Pop-up Books

### Bollmann's Map of New York

Hermann Bollmann's acclaimed bird's-eye view of New York City is one of over sixty such city maps by this cartographer, although most were produced for European cities. The map is undated, but is probably no later than 1966. For it Bollmann's staff designed and built special cameras and took about 67,000 individual photographs of which about 17,000 were shot from the air. Published by Bollmann Bildkarten Verlag, the map was drawn by hand with great accuracy down to the smallest detail.

The simulation of three-dimensional objects in space dates back to the early Renaissance, when painters searched for, and eventually formulated, a set of rules for constructing realistic spatial settings which became known as perspective. These rules derived from a study of optics and the changes which occur in our perception of horizontal and vertical elements over increasing distances. They were equally applicable to the transposition of architects' plans and elevations into three-dimensional volumes which could be constructed from any viewpoint; a contemporary example of this usage is the bird's-eye-view city map by Hermann Bollmann [1]. Besides using perspective, architects developed a number of specialized methods for presenting their designs such as isometric and axonometric constructions.

The creation of technical drawings takes a great deal of time, and it was only with the arrival of the computer and sophisticated modelling programs that architects were able to present their buildings not only from any viewpoint – both internally and externally – but also in a form which enabled the viewer to move around and through their designs. The latter three-dimensional experience had previously only been possible once a building had been completed, of course. Similar expertise became available to product designers through programs intended to model any colour or surface texture of a proposed design from plans and elevations. One of the outcomes of these programs and the introduction of computer-aided design or modelling (CAD/CAM) techniques was to enable complete products on any scale to be designed, stress-tested and manufactured without using paper-based plans or drawings at all.

Three-dimensional computer modelling has been used to interesting effect in museums and

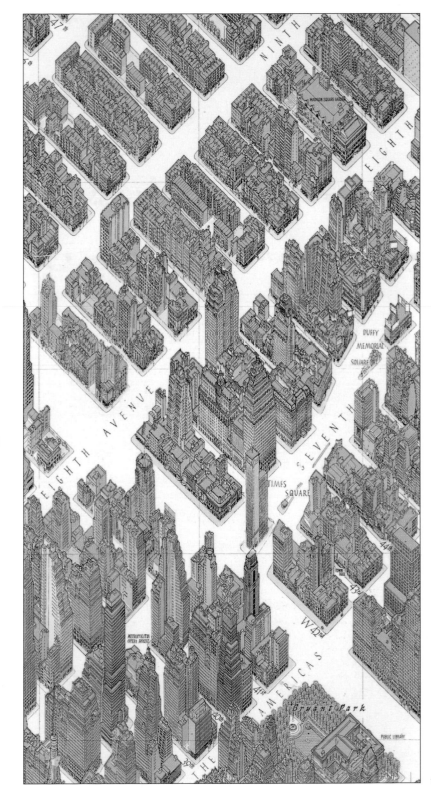

galleries. Because they need to be protected from visitors, objects exhibited in traditional settings can only present an unvarying succession of static layouts in showcases to their viewers. With the introduction of digital display techniques, valuable or environmentally sensitive artefacts have been replaced with holograms and video displays which make it possible to experience them in the round.

Exhibition design, like museum installation design, evolved to display objects on a variety of scales. Multimedia in an exhibition context implies the coming together of a variety of different media in order to tell a particular story. These media might include text, photographs, multi-screen presentations, slide shows, film, sound and lighting. The best such exhibitions are dramatic events in which the visitor participates actively, coming away with much the same satisfaction as from a visit to the theatre. Of particular interest

1

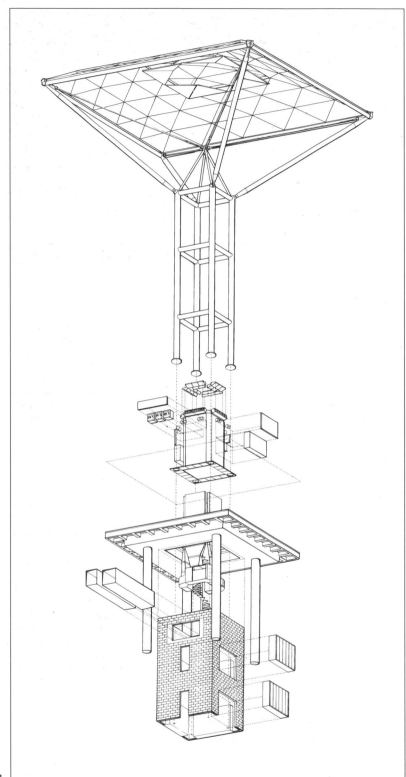

were the imaginative exhibitions designed by Will Burtin, who emigrated from Germany to the U.S.A. in 1938 and who was known as the art director of *Fortune* magazine. During the 1950s and '60s, Burtin's office specialized in the visualization and popularization of scientific information through exhibitions. The human cell and brain were two of the first subjects to be explored from the inside via multimedia presentations [3]. Of comparable importance were the exhibition designs from the same period by Charles and Ray Eames which included *Glimpses of the U.S.A.*, a giant multi-screen presentation designed for Moscow in 1959, *Mathematica* at the California Museum of Science and Industry, Los Angeles, in 1960, and an international travelling exhibition, *The World of Franklin and Jefferson*. A number of contemporary exhibitions and museum displays have carried on this tradition, aided by digital technology which provides interactive databases and video and text components.

One of the practical problems of combining film or video in any spatial format has been the conflict between the almost compulsive attraction of the moving image, coupled with sound, over all forms of static presentation. A sound track can be heard over a large area unless some form of personal listening device is used, and it can effectively prevent text from being read elsewhere in an exhibition. Wherever film or video is shown within an exhibition, visitors will collect to view the screen until the sequence ends. Inevitably, there is congestion, and the number of visitors at any one time has to be limited. This means that the moving image either has to be shown in a separate, sound-proof area or used in silent mode along with other exhibits.

Electronic, multimedia-based exhibitions can provide an unrivalled source of information, although the small size of monitors can limit the number of people able to view them at any one time. Such shows are often unable to provide the variety of scale or drama which is inherent in a real-time exhibit, however. Virtual reality (VR) could make a huge difference in this regard. At the moment, VR suffers, as did the stereo cinema film, from the inconvenience of the viewer having to wear special equipment. Flight simulators can provide interactive experiences without special equipment but at enormous cost.

Given the amount of attention focused on developments in the area of computer technology, it might come as a surprise that printed books can still delight us as successful examples of three-dimensional presentation. The stereo image, although limited by its red/green spectacles, has been sucessfully used to demonstrate a series of geometrical constructions in a school text book. Children's pop-up books (pp. 146–47 [1–3]) have provided entertaining 3-D constructions which go beyond what is possible with flat imagery. Many of the popular how-do-they-work books offer interesting simulated 3-D through their exploded diagram treatments (pp. 144–45), which utilize both photography and drawn illustrations.

The ease with which 3-D computer simulations can be created has led to some notable new visual treatments for describing the structure and contents of software programs. The traditional two-dimensional 'family tree' has been transformed into a three-dimensional construct using a series of small angled screens stacked up one behind the other to display the sequence in which screens fall along a timeline and their interconnections with other pathways within the system (p. 133 [7]). This schematic has proved valuable in providing master 'contents' lists for complex works such as on-screen encyclopaedias.

3

Another interesting development has come from the Visible Language Workshop at the Massachusetts Institute of Technology in Boston, which has 'liberated' text from the flat surface of the monitor screen and projected it into simulated space as clusters of 'text blocks' floating in front of the viewer. The user is encouraged to navigate through this space by means of context, colour, standard typographic hierarchies of size and weight, and positioning of text. The late Muriel Cooper coined the term 'Information Landscape' to describe this new method of presenting information, one in which a broad overview 'contains' various blocks of text seen in the middle and far distance. Each alternative can be 'zoomed in' to the foreground with further alternatives coming into view 'behind' it. It is difficult to describe the effectiveness of this technique by means of static images. It has been applied to a range of subject-matter as diverse as town and city maps, financial diagrams and newspaper content. Digital exploration of virtual space is clearly becoming the new frontier of information design.

### Architectural Drawing

An exploded axonometric drawing of a central structure at Stansted Airport (near London), designed by Foster and Partners, clearly shows how the complex three-dimensional relationship of components fit together.

### The Upjohn *Brain Exhibit*

Will Burtin's first major exhibition success was a twenty-four-foot-diameter interpretation of a human cell for the Upjohn Company in America. The *Brain Exhibit* of 1960 [3] developed the concept further and anticipated large multimedia events including projected images, light and colour. It was a dramatic visualization of the structure of the human brain on a scale never previously attempted.

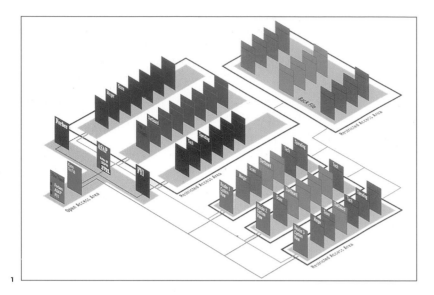

1

**1 – 5**

**Dynamic Diagrams**

Dynamic Diagrams are one of the leaders in the structural planning of web sites, which includes typography, visual programs, navigational systems and grouping of information. Visualizing information structure is an important stage in the web-site design process; discussions with the client are transformed into planning diagrams capturing the logical groupings of information in a visual form. These planning diagrams in turn become the basis for further discussion, leading to the creation of a site map such as that for *Britannica On Line*.
*Design: Dynamic Diagrams, U.S.A.*

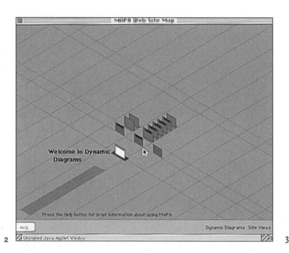

2

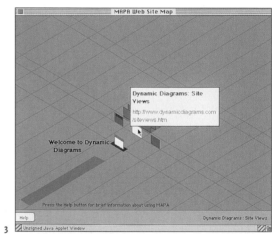

3

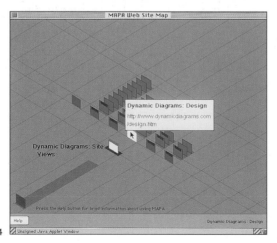

4

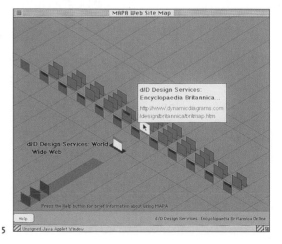

5

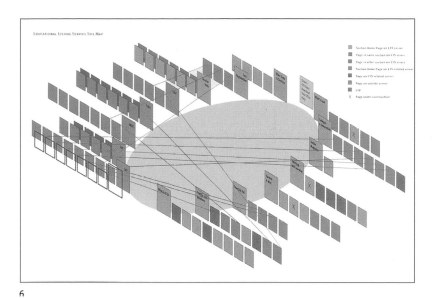

EDUCATIONAL TESTING SERVICE SITE MAP

The *Britannica On Line* web site was designed in 1996. Its goal was to bring clarity and accessibility to a reference classic already being used by several million people. The screen design accommodates the text and graphics generated from a hundred thousand articles. The splash page design emphasizes the division of the *Britannica* into two distinct areas: the free public side (in yellow) and the subscriber section (in green). By mirroring the structure, the free pages make the visitor aware of the rich features available to paid subscribers, encouraging use of the free trial.
*Design: Dynamic Diagrams, U.S.A.*

● Virtual Space

133

6

7

**1 – 6**

**Sensorium Web Site**

Sensorium is an experimental, alternative 'digital museum' designed to create a 'public sensory platform on the Net'. The project was originally conceived as the Japanese theme pavilion at IWE96 (Internet World Exposition), the first global expo on the Net; in 1997, it received the Golden Nica prize at the Ars Electronica festival in Linz. The Sensorium was set up to convey experiences which would be unique to the Net; one of its inspirations was the book *Powers of Ten* (p. 57). *Breathing Earth*, one of the site's applications, shows by means of loop-animation the earthquakes which have occurred across the globe during the previous fourteen days. The contents take the form of a web site filmed by means of time-lapse photography augmented by on-line data from the International Database Centre (IDC). *Design: Yoshiaki Nishimura, Japan*

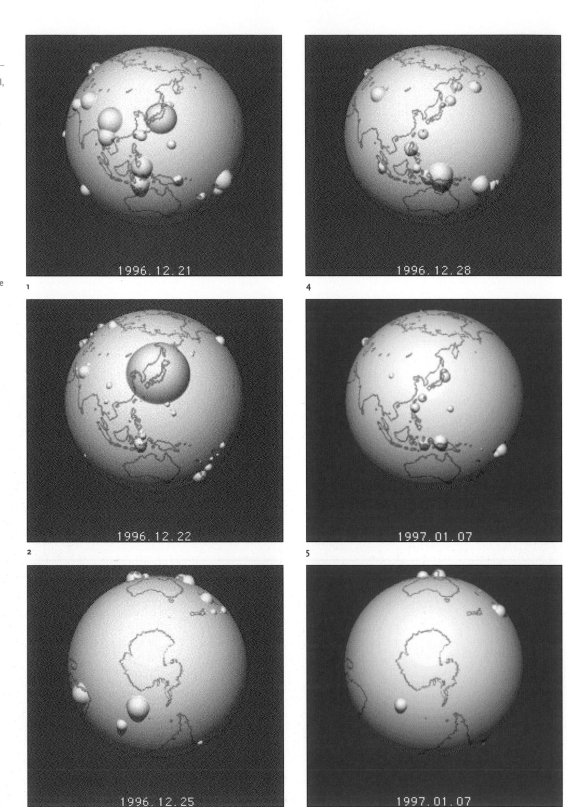

1   1996.12.21

2   1996.12.22

3   1996.12.25

4   1996.12.28

5   1997.01.07

6   1997.01.07

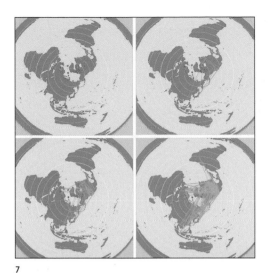

7

**7 – 8
Web Hopper**

Web Hopper is a web site offering real-time visualization of global web traffic as observed from the network operation centre at Keio University in Japan. It enables Internet users to visualize their web-hopping and that of other Net users. The interface represents your trail of links crossing the world as a red line and those of other users as blue lines. Web Hopper translates http (hypertext transfer protocol) information about web site addresses into latitude and longitude co-ordinates by passing the data through the network operation centre; the system refers in real time to a database on the 'Host Name to Latitude/Longitude' page at Illinois University. This information is then rendered on screen using an application written in the JAVA programming language.
*Design: Yoshiaki Nishimura, Japan*

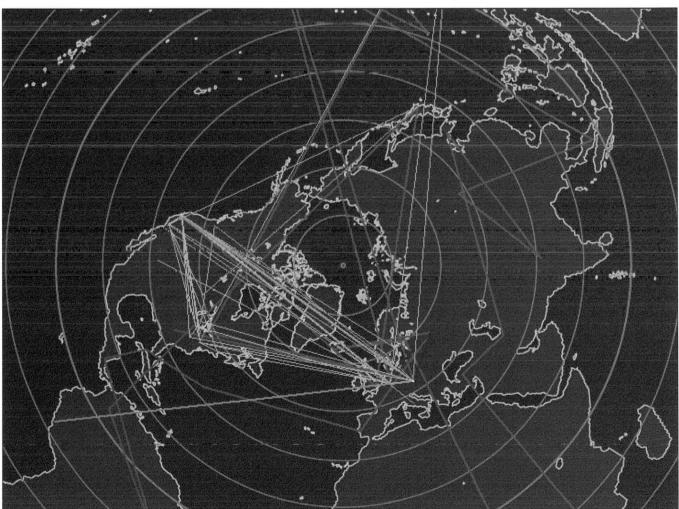

8

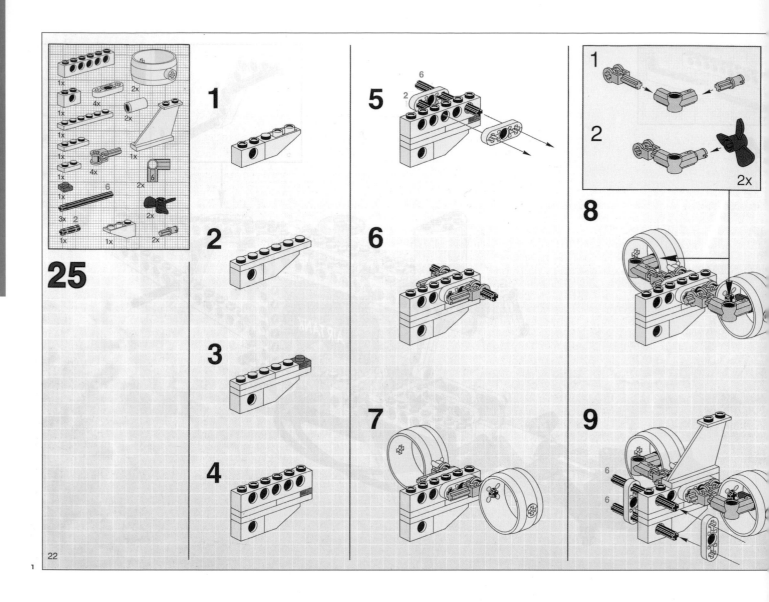

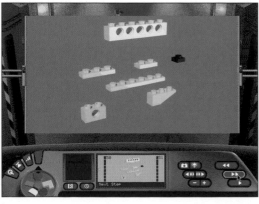

**1**

LEGO **Assembly Manual**

This LEGO 'Technic' assembly manual is supplied in two different formats: a conventional printed manual [1] and an interactive CD-ROM [**2 – 5**]. The printed manual, a model of its kind, describes in sixteen pages the step-by-step assembly of a kit, in this instance a working-model submersible complete with diver.

2

3

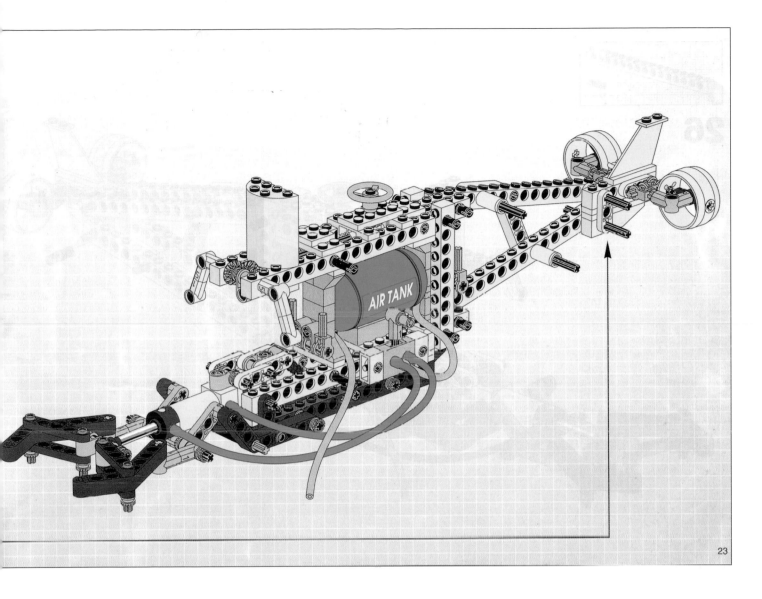

AIR TANK

23

4

5

**2 – 5**
**LEGO Assembly Manual**

The CD-ROM version of the instructions provides a short, printed user's guide as well as an on-screen control panel which activates a number of functions of the build program as well as providing detailed background information about submersibles and underwater life in general.
*Concept and design: The LEGO Group, Denmark*

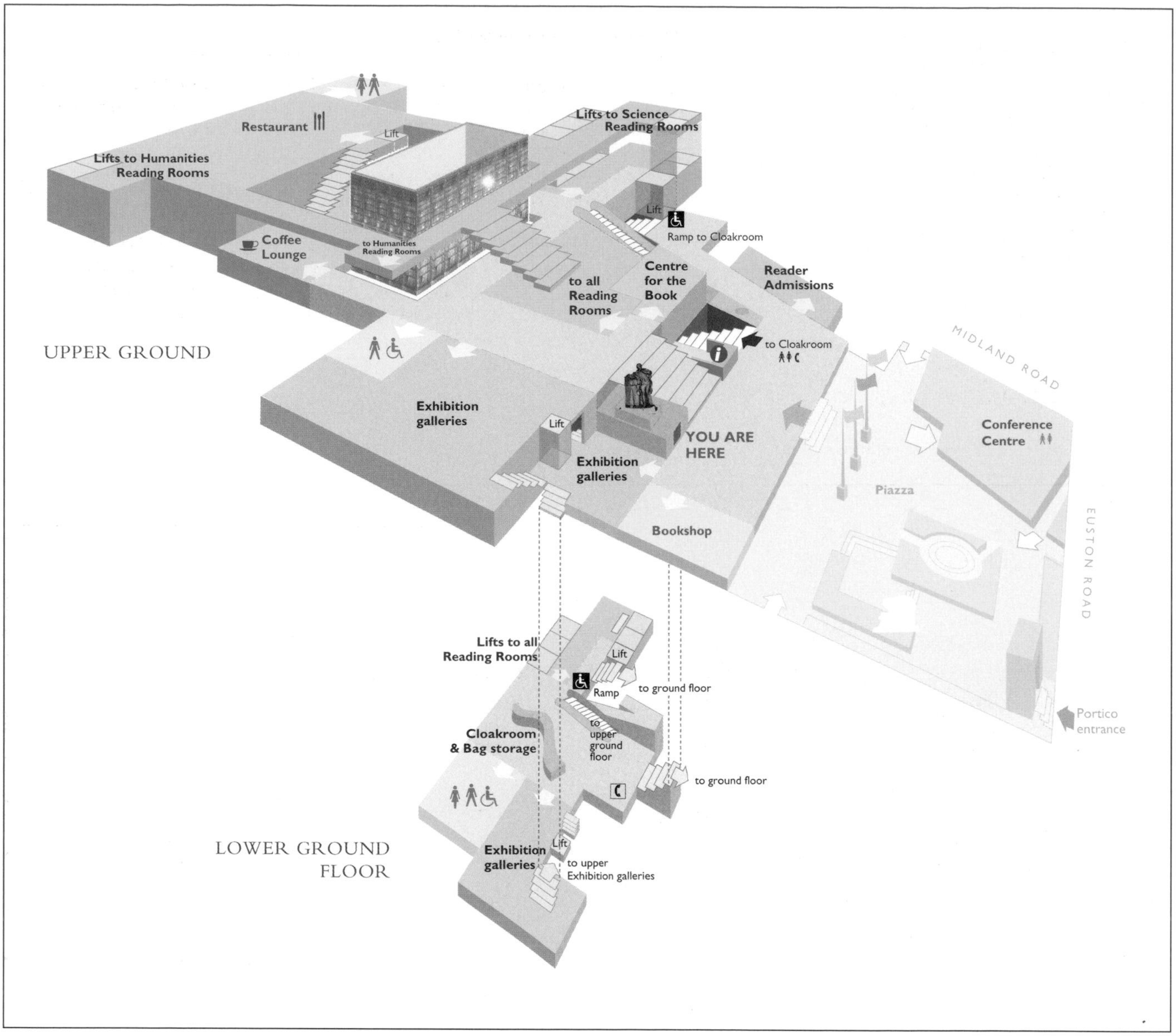

Restaurant

Lifts to Humanities
Reading Rooms

Lifts to Science
Reading Rooms

Lift

Coffee
Lounge

to Humanities
Reading Rooms

Lift

Ramp to Cloakroom

to all
Reading
Rooms

Centre
for the
Book

Reader
Admissions

MIDLAND ROAD

UPPER GROUND

to Cloakroom

Exhibition
galleries

Lift

Conference
Centre

YOU ARE
HERE

Piazza

Exhibition
galleries

EUSTON ROAD

Bookshop

Lifts to all
Reading Rooms

Lift

Ramp

to ground floor

Portico
entrance

Cloakroom
& Bag storage

to
upper
ground
floor

to ground floor

LOWER GROUND
FLOOR

Exhibition
galleries

Lift

to upper
Exhibition galleries

## 1 – 3
### British Library Orientation Diagrams

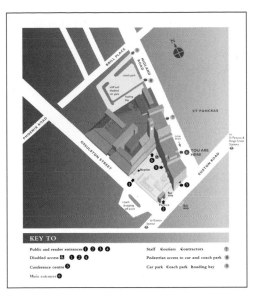

2

These orientation diagrams for the new British Library in Kings Cross, London, were based largely on architectural plans and discussions with the architects, Colin St John Wilson & Partners. The diagrams simplify the complex spaces to help people create mental models of the buildings and the areas accessible to them. The site plan [2] shows key information (entrances, roads, etc.) for people arriving at the Library. The three-dimensional orientation diagrams [1, 3], created in Adobe Illustrator, are two-point perspectives drawn from an angle carefully selected to show all areas of the building. In the diagrams which illustrate the public and reading areas, the glass-clad tower of leather-bound books (Kings Library) is used as a prominent landmark to help users orientate themselves.
*Design: Colette Miller, Information Design Unit, u.k.*

3

# Neighbourhood Maps for the Blind
## Finding the Way by Ear, Hand and Foot

The visually impaired are partially or completely cut off from sighted people's most essential contact with the world around them. Visual impairment greatly limits orientation and mobility as well as the many types of experiences that come principally through sight. Having become aware of this, the Danish Design Centre chose as its first design research challenge a project with the working title of 'Maps for the Blind'. The project was implemented with funds made available by the Danish Ministry of Industry from the sale of silver coins minted for the fiftieth birthday of Her Majesty the Queen.

The project's primary purpose was to develop city maps and other systems to provide information about places and directions to the blind and partially sighted. The goal was to develop tactile maps based on individual needs, edited in CAD and produced in runs as small as one copy. But no maps for the blind can solve the problems that they solve for sighted people, and that realization sparked a new goal: to create an electronic, voice-controlled navigator for the visually impaired. A third goal was to work on the city itself and develop a system of tactile paving stones.

At the outset, a series of scenarios was devised to illustrate how people with severe visual impairment get around and what they experience along the way. These scenarios were used to determine precise requirements in the three different areas: relief maps, electronic systems and changes in the physical city.

The first phase of the project was implemented in collaboration with the consultant engineering company Micro Consult. In this phase, the Danish Design Centre collected basic information about the needs of the blind and partially sighted in consultation with the Danish Blind Association, the Institute for the Blind and Partially Sighted, and visually impaired people who provided assistance on an individual basis. The Danish Design Centre also made contact with researchers, engineers and institutions in Europe, the U.S.A.,

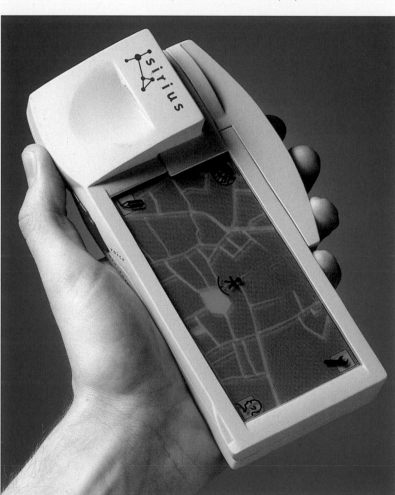

1

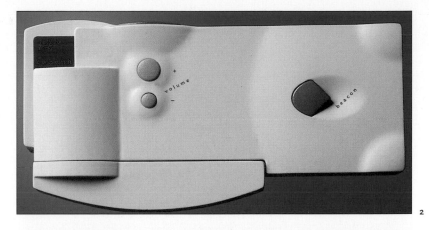

2

3

Australia and Japan. This process provided a picture of what was happening globally and suggested avenues to explore. Micro Consult investigated ways of using various types of new electronic technology for place and direction orientation, and the Danish Design Centre sought collaboration with two of the country's leading city planning and landscape architects.

The next phase of the project was aimed at developing models and fully worked-out solutions. This was done together with selected industrial companies which were able to take the results of the work from the research phase and convert them into products.

The blind typically know places in a city through the routes and the means of transport they use to get to them. But even if the way is known from a given departure point, a blind person often will not know where specific places are in relation to one another. A tactile relief map is one of the only non-verbal ways for the blind to get a real feeling for this, provided, of course, that it has been made to a suitable scale, contains relevant information and is based on symbols with which the blind are familiar. The first phase of the project outlined a number of possibilities here, and, in addition, there was the development of methods for data registration. The aim was to make it economically feasible to produce city maps according to individual needs in print runs as small as one copy.

All over the world, there are a number of electronic systems either being developed or already being used that could be utilized by the blind and partially sighted with small alterations or in new combinations. The aim was to demonstrate how one or more of these systems could be adapted to the Danish Design Centre's purposes and to outline the development work necessary.

Finally, the design research project was concerned with the design of the physical environment itself. The purpose was to make the city friendlier, more comprehensible and richer in experiences. One of the subjects with which the project was concerned was the use of tactile pavement areas which would make it possible

1 – 3

The Sirius navigator, which is still under development, uses the GPS global positioning system with an accuracy that will enable it to show which side of the street the user is on as well as identify a house number. It will set up a route plan on its touch-sensitive screen and will have a synthetic speech output facility as well as a built-in mobile telephone unit. The controls are clearly differentiated; only one of the buttons has two functions.

A simplified route plan can be called up on the Sirius screen.

for the blind and partially sighted to 'read' useful information literally through the soles of their feet, using either new types of pavement or already familiar pavement considered in new ways. The project also dealt with how the city could contribute to a rich experience when accessed through all the senses. Methods developed to make the city more friendly for the blind and partially sighted would benefit every user.

All three aspects have now been tested by many different types of user. CAD/CAM maps are being produced, and there are plans to make them available in special manuals for individual use. Tactile paving stones are in production and are being specified by planners and architects in several cities in Denmark. The possibilities of the electronic navigator are being investigated, and we see great potential in the fact that it is voice-controlled and therefore of use to those without visual impairment such as sighted visitors and tourists.     *Birgitta Capetillo*

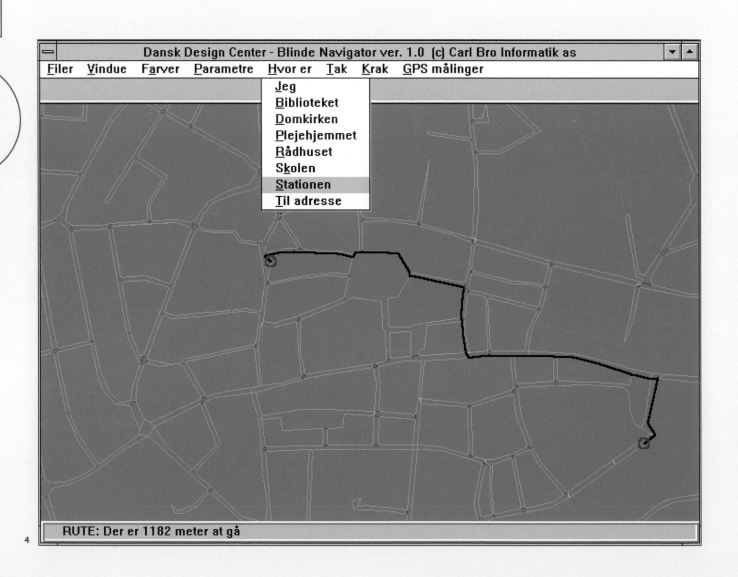

Dansk Design Center – Blinde Navigator ver. 1.0 (c) Carl Bro Informatik as

Filer   Vindue   Farver   Parametre   Hvor er   Tak   Krak   GPS målinger

Jeg
Biblioteket
Domkirken
Plejehjemmet
Rådhuset
Skolen
Stationen
Til adresse

RUTE: Der er 1182 meter at gå

4

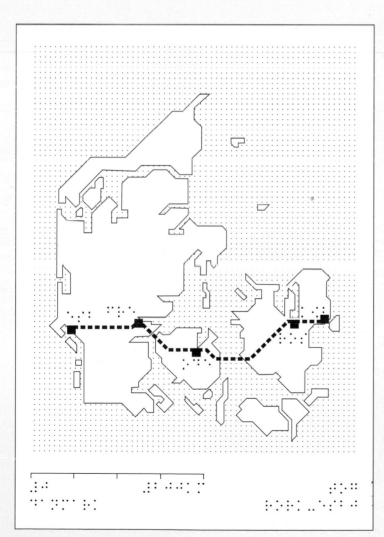

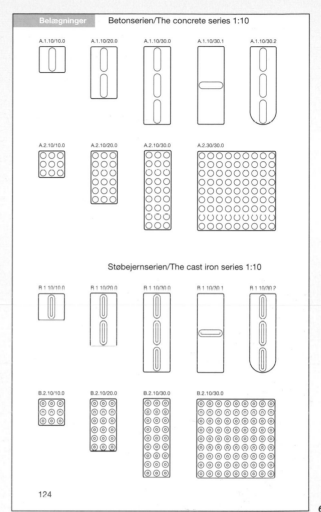

**5 – 6**

[5] shows one of a number of
tactile (embossed) maps
produced at different scales
with a braille explanation at
the foot of the page. A tactile
paving system [6] is planned
which will be able to
communicate a whole range
of pavement 'information'
such as crossing points,
entries to buildings, post-
boxes and bus-stops.

1

**Exploded Diagram of Westland Helicopter**

A spread from *Stephen Biesty's Incredible Cross-Sections*, first published in 1992, is shown here without its text. This book features eighteen large, three-dimensional representations of complex machines and buildings ranging from the Space Shuttle to a cathedral. These highly detailed, cross-sectional illustrations, a treatment usually reserved for describing the technical workings of vehicles and machinery, are highly effective in revealing the interaction of people with complex systems like multi-level subway stations or opera houses as used simultaneously by performers and audiences. In each case, the inclusion of to-scale figures humanizes the drawing. One is never left with the impression that these are purely technical representations, although each subject has been meticulously researched for accuracy. The subject shown here is the Westland Sea King helicopter in its air-sea rescue livery. *Illustration: Stephen Biesty; publisher: Dorling Kindersley, u.k.*

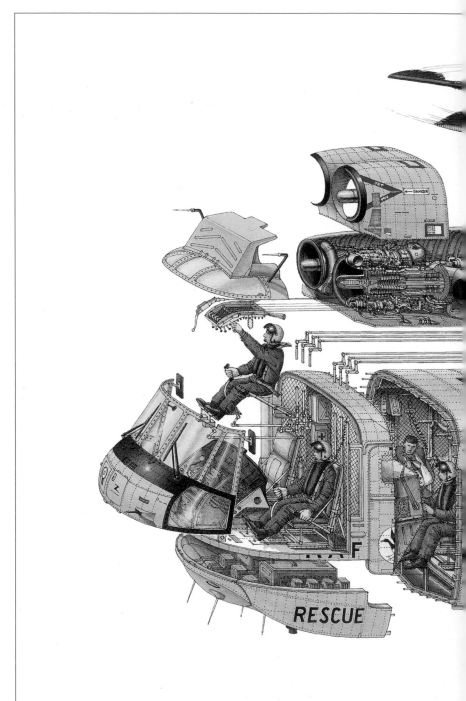

1

1

2

**1 – 3**

**Van der Meer 3-D Packs**

The subjects of these pop-up packs (produced in book format) were carefully chosen by the publisher so that the content of each one would be enhanced by three-dimensional presentation. The two packs shown, *The Architecture Pack* [1,3] and *The Brain Pack* [2], illustrate both the astonishing complexity of their paper engineering and the interactive elements in many of the spreads. They underline the publisher's claim to provide instruction and entertainment for the broadest possible audience.

Designer Ron van der Meer quotes a Chinese proverb ('To hear is to forget, to see is to remember, to do is to understand') in support of his unique approach to these interactive books. Some of the packs took as much as two years to discuss and produce; all involved close collaboration between an author, a researcher and the designer, who is both paper engineer and graphic designer. The pop-up constructions were modelled in white paper to establish their functionality as well as to assess cost and ease of

assembly. Only then did the projects proceed with authors writing to fit available spaces and the designer preparing the graphics. A special paper was used, and its grain was taken into account to make the pop-up structures as rigid as possible. The complex and delicate assembly work was carried out in China or Colombia.
*Concept: Ron van der Meer, U.K.; design and paper engineering: Corina Fletcher and Mark Hiner; publisher: Van der Meer®, a division of PHPC and Co.*

# 6 Mapping the Internal and External Worlds

Strip Maps • Road Atlases • Upside-down Maps • Distribution Maps • Invisible Information

**Pilgrim Map**

An early pilgrim map based on the strip-map principle shows only the main route together with prominent landmarks, in this case churches and religious establishments. It is reputed to have been drawn by the monk Matthew Paris.

Most people find it impossible to throw a map away; maps are such concentrated sources of information, and frequently so attractive graphically, that they are often treasured even when they become outdated. Today's maps often contain many layers of information and are accurate over their entire areas. This has not always been the case. On early maps and charts, accuracy was only to be found in limited areas, generally those between towns and cities (in the case of land maps) and along coastlines (in the case of sea charts). Early mapmakers were extremely inventive, combining fact and myth in about equal proportions, and their maps were meant to be used as guides to landmarks along established routes [1]. Today we think of maps as being in the public domain, but so valuable was the information contained in early sea charts that they were often kept secret by those who owned them.

The great period of mapmaking coincided with the age of European exploration of other continents, and maps from this time can best be described as tokens of territorial claim. Discovery of a new coastline was not enough to secure a claim on a map; the area could only be filled in with the appropriate colour if an entire land mass could be defined, whether it turned out to be an island or a continent. Perhaps the greatest challenge during this period was accuracy of presentation. The problem of converting information from the curved surface of a spherical planet to a two-dimensional map surface remained a difficult one. It was relatively easy to achieve accuracy in certain key areas of information, such as the distance between towns, compass directions or the general shapes of land masses, but almost impossible to achieve all three together in one map. The history of mapmaking has really been a quest to overcome this.

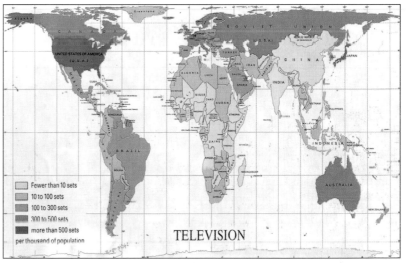

VERZERRUNG DURCH
MERCATOR-PROJEKTION

Nach Dozent Dr. Karl Peucker

Gesellschafts- und Wirtschaftsmuseum in Wien
Deutscher Verlag für Jugend und Volk, Ges. m. b. H., Wien, I.
Druck: Laurenz Schlager, Wien, VII.
Neurath, Bildstatistik

Tafel XVI

**2**

Fewer than 10 sets
10 to 100 sets
100 to 300 sets
300 to 500 sets
more than 500 sets
per thousand of population

TELEVISION

**3**

As an example of the distortion which can be produced in trying to 'project' a spherical object (the earth) on to a flat rectangular surface, we can take the example of Gerhardus Mercator's world projection, which is still in widespread use today, but which produces an increasing amount of distortion as one moves further north or south of a mid-position. A dramatic illustration of this distortion is an isotype diagram of the '30s which shows the silhouette of a man placed next to the same image as it would have looked if plotted on the basis of Mercator's system [2].

Mapping has been transformed by satellite and digital techniques with seemingly unlimited possibilities for accuracy, definition and areas of coverage. But there seems to have been no comparable advance in the typographical detailing of many maps, particularly in the methods used for coping with the annotation of very small areas and the problems of dealing with a high density of place names. One solution has been the adoption of the screen-based technique of typographical information.

Amongst map types, one of the longest-lived is the strip map, of which examples date back to Roman times. From medieval times onwards, examples of this type are plentiful [1], as are contemporary ones(p. 154). Even in more leisurely ages than our own, there was probably little to interest the traveller than the most direct route to

**Projections of the World**

Traditional world-map projections such as Mercator's [2] tend to show countries with inaccurate relative proportions, which Arno Peters' more recent project [3] attempts to rectify. This map from the *Compact Peters' Atlas of the World* shows his projections as the base for a representation of world-wide TV ownership. *Courtesy Addison Wesley Longman Ltd, U.K.*

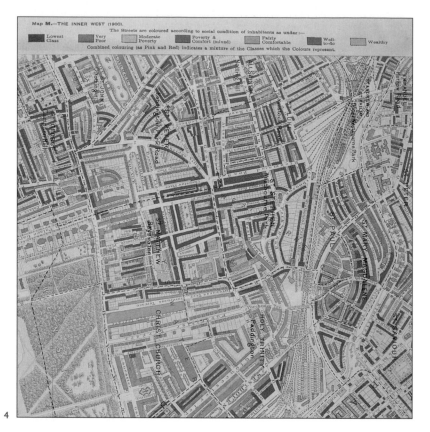

Map M.—THE INNER WEST (1900).
The Streets are coloured according to social condition of inhabitants as under:—

Lowest Class | Very Poor | Moderate Poverty | Poverty & Comfort (mixed) | Fairly Comfortable | Well-to-do | Wealthy

Combined colouring (as Pink and Red) indicates a mixture of the Classes which the Colours represent.

4

**Charles Booth's Map of London Poverty**

The colour key to the Charles Booth map illustrated on page 11 shows whole streets and, in some cases, individual houses colour-coded using a scale of seven colours ranging from dark blue (representing the 'lowest class') through purple ('poverty and comfort') to yellow (the 'wealthy').

his or her destination. As a result, strip maps took on most of the characteristics of network maps, which ignore scale altogether. An interesting type of strip map is the upside-down map which caters for drivers requiring a format which can be read in both directions of travel with equal facility. All of the typographical entries are repeated in inverted form, thus eliminating the necessity of turning the map around to read place names and road numbers (p. 148 [1]). A further refinement is a complete road atlas which can be read in the same manner (pp. 158–59 [1–4]).

The first world map of real use to navigators was that devised in the sixteenth century by the Flemish cartographer Mercator. In the early 1940s, Buckminster Fuller produced his Dymaxion Air-Ocean map, although an earlier version dates from 1927. This attempt to reduce distortion of the world map gave near-equality of area and distance along Great Circle arc segments. The international airlines emerging at the time made use of this map when planning their new intercontinental routes. During the 1970s, Arno Peters, a German cartographer with strong socialist views, launched a new world-map projection aimed at reconciling the various problems associated with earlier ones, in particular the challenge of accurately defining the sizes of the major continents [3]. Peters's projection, though factually accurate, has not proven to be very popular, and it remains to be seen whether it will overcome our cultural conservatism, which is based on Mercator's inaccurate projection. Whilst it has been relatively easy to accept a new image of Planet Earth in the form of satellite views from outer space, it seems difficult to modify our memory of school-book atlases to match topographical reality.

The majority of maps are concerned with accuracy of measurement: they have fixed scales which relate to distances on the ground, colour conventions, and codes for the sizes of population centres. An entirely different sort of map has evolved during this century which has none of these characteristics. It is not to scale, the distance between regularly spaced destinations is not equal, and the map does not relate to any observable landmarks, with only the most generalized relation to the compass. This is the network map, a map we use everyday for travelling on the Underground or planning flights. Its sole purpose is to tell us the sequence of stops and the possibility of making interchange connections along any given route. One interesting amplification of this type is a map recently designed for the Buenos Aires metro which successfully integrates the underground network with a formalized street-level plan (pp. 46–47 [1–5]).

Probably the most interesting cartographic development of the past twenty years is the use of the map concept to communicate a whole range of cultural, economic and predictive information about the world. Building on the public's familiarity with map conventions and the map's reputation for accuracy, this new concept has embraced such diverse subjects as human languages (pp. 162–63) and the presence of dangers to human life. An early precurser of this type of map is Charles Booth's map [4] showing, by means of a seven-part colour scale, the distribution of wealth and poverty in late nineteenth-century London. An early example, if not the earliest, of a predictive map is Edmund Halley's for 22 April 1715 in which he graphically predicted 'the passage of the shadow of the moon over England' [5]. The most frequently used predictive map is, of course, the weather map which now regularly appears in all media on a daily – sometimes an hourly – basis. Interestingly, weather maps are often presented in two forms: a synoptic map for the 'professional' user – the farmer, the sailor or the pilot – which requires a certain amount of interpretation, and a simpler version for the general public in the form of a pictographic presentation.

The mapping concept has proven so effective that map formats are being used to delineate not only the geographical world but also those of biology and industry. Such maps rely entirely on digital techniques and various forms of body imaging developed over the past decade. This area – the opposite of space exploration – promises to be the next great frontier for investigation by information designers.

5

**A Predictive Map**

Edmund Halley, the eighteenth-century astronomer, created this predictive map for the eclipse of the sun on 22 April 1715. An eclipse was a frightening experience for most of the population at this time. .

**Risk Map**

Mark Monmonier, author of the 1997 book *Cartographies of Danger*, has written: 'This dot map strikes a visually effective compromise by representing only locations at which tornadoes first touched down, rather than the direction and length of their paths. To avoid graphic clutter in high risk areas, a single dot represents an average location for two tornadoes.' *Publisher: The University of Chicago Press, U.S.A*

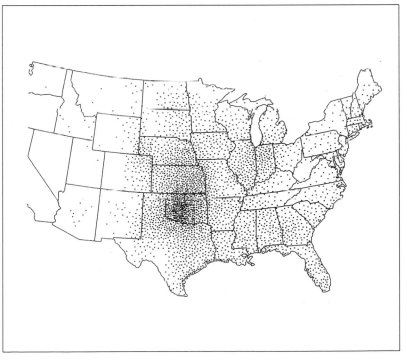

6

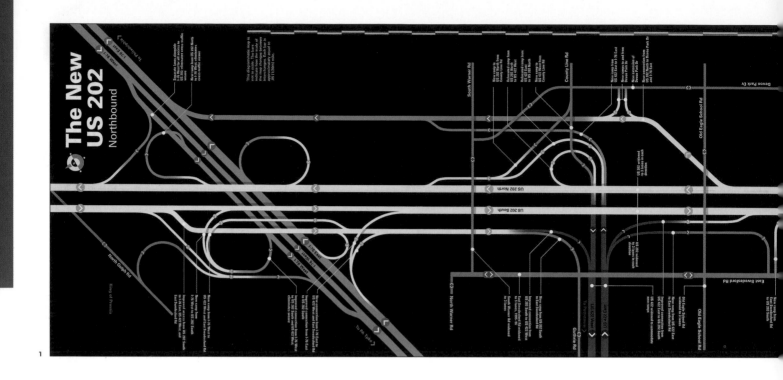

1

**Penn DOT Map**

This map of U.S. 202 for the Pennsylvania Department of Transportation folds down to 4 × 9 inches and out to 35 ¹/₂ inches as a complete strip-map. It shows the changes being made to a 4-¹/₄-mile stretch of a busy suburban route and an extremely congested interchange. This bi-directional map shows both north–south and, when turned around, south–north routings and repeats typography for both directions. Colour coding is used to distinguish different road types.
*Design and electronic cartography: Joel Katz, U.S.A.*

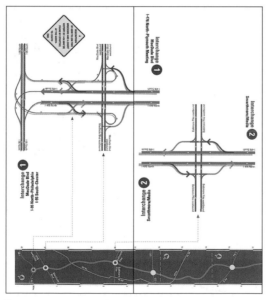

2

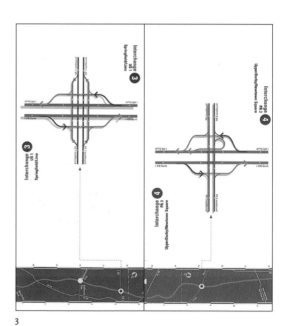

3

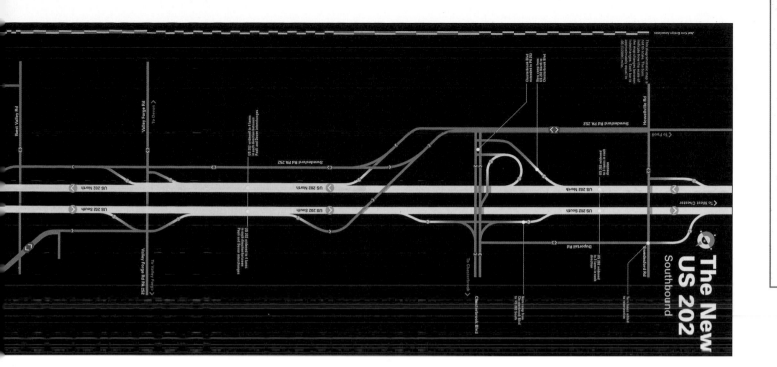

The New
US 202
Southbound

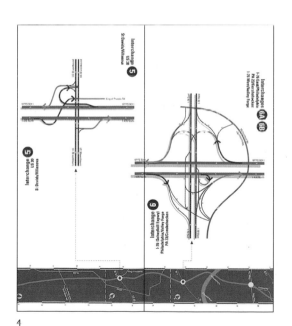

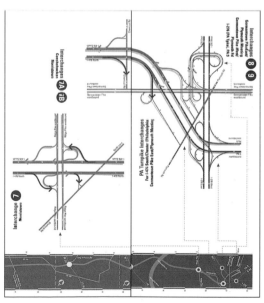

4

5

2–5
## u.s. Interstate 476 Maps

Although it also utilizes the
strip-map principle, this map
of Interstate 476 takes the
form of a conventional
stapled brochure. The strip-
map runs continuously along
the lower edge and is used
to place the complex
interchange diagrams
(some with three layers)
in context. This enables the
diagrams to be shown large
while keeping the format to
4 × 9 inches. The brochure
is held horizontally and
paged through from the top.
One way is north–south,
the other south–north.
The interchange diagrams
read in both directions.
Colour differentiates road
types and exits.
*Design and electronic
cartography: Joel Katz, u.s.a.*

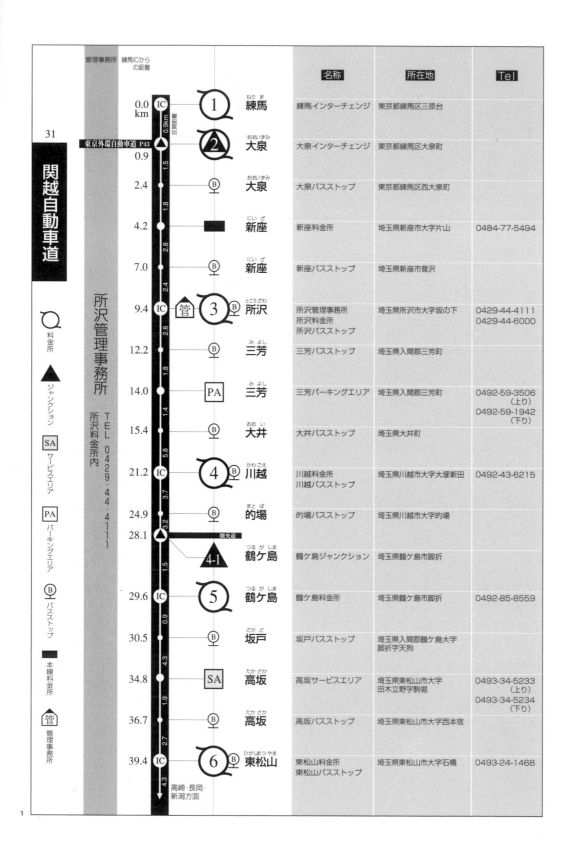

関越自動車道

31

所沢管理事務所
所沢料金所内
TEL 0429・44・4111

| | 名称 | 所在地 | Tel |
|---|---|---|---|
| ① 練馬 (ねりま) | 練馬インターチェンジ | 東京都練馬区三原台 | |
| ② 大泉 (おおいずみ) | 大泉インターチェンジ | 東京都練馬区大泉町 | |
| Ⓑ 大泉 (おおいずみ) | 大泉バスストップ | 東京都練馬区西大泉町 | |
| ■ 新座 (にいざ) | 新座料金所 | 埼玉県新座市大字片山 | 0484-77-5494 |
| Ⓑ 新座 (にいざ) | 新座バスストップ | 埼玉県新座市菅沢 | |
| ③ 所沢 (ところざわ) | 所沢管理事務所 所沢料金所 所沢バスストップ | 埼玉県所沢市大字坂の下 | 0429-44-4111 0429-44-6000 |
| Ⓑ 三芳 (みよし) | 三芳バスストップ | 埼玉県入間郡三芳町 | |
| PA 三芳 (みよし) | 三芳パーキングエリア | 埼玉県入間郡三芳町 | 0492-59-3506 (上り) 0492-59-1942 (下り) |
| Ⓑ 大井 (おおい) | 大井バスストップ | 埼玉県大井町 | |
| ④ 川越 (かわごえ) | 川越料金所 川越バスストップ | 埼玉県川越市大字大塚新田 | 0492-43-6215 |
| Ⓑ 的場 (まとば) | 的場バスストップ | 埼玉県川越市大字的場 | |
| 4-1 鶴ケ島 (つるがしま) | 鶴ケ島ジャンクション | 埼玉県鶴ケ島市脚折 | |
| ⑤ 鶴ケ島 (つるがしま) | 鶴ケ島料金所 | 埼玉県鶴ケ島市脚折 | 0492-85-8559 |
| Ⓑ 坂戸 (さかど) | 坂戸バスストップ | 埼玉県入間郡鶴ケ島大字脚折字天狗 | |
| SA 高坂 (たかさか) | 高坂サービスエリア | 埼玉県東松山市大字田木立野字駒堀 | 0493-34-5233 (上り) 0493-34-5234 (下り) |
| Ⓑ 高坂 (たかさか) | 高坂バスストップ | 埼玉県東松山市大字西本宿 | |
| ⑥ 東松山 (ひがしまつやま) | 東松山料金所 東松山バスストップ | 埼玉県東松山市大字石橋 | 0493-24-1468 |

管理事務所 練馬ICからの距離

0.0 km
0.9
2.4
4.2
7.0
9.4
12.2
14.0
15.4
21.2
24.9
28.1
29.6
30.5
34.8
36.7
39.4

東京外環自動車道 P43
圏央道
高崎・長岡・新潟方面

Ｑ 料金所
▲ ジャンクション
SA サービスエリア
PA パーキングエリア
Ⓑ バスストップ
■ 本線料金所
管 管理事務所

**1**

**Japanese Highway Handbook**

The comprehensive 1996 handbook of the Japanese highway system consists of ninety-six pages of statistical information about facilities and distances, as well as relevant addresses and telephone numbers.
It also includes a ten-page section of strip-maps which use a range of symbols to convey information about major interchanges, toll gates, parking, maintenance facilities and restaurants.
In case of a serious accident, the exact location and distance from the nearest facilities can be determined immediately.
*Design: Hiroyuki Kimura, Tube Graphics, Japan*

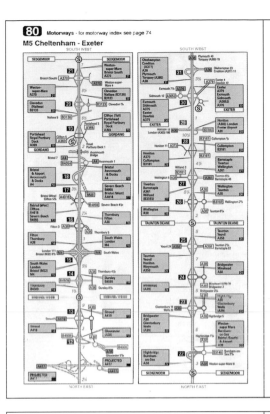

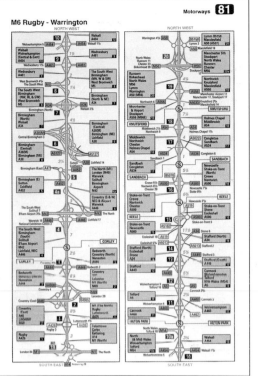

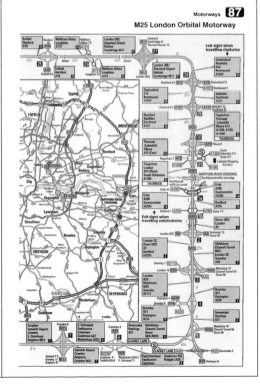

2 – 3
AA Motorway Handbook

The English Automobile Association (AA) has for many years included in its members' handbook a section on the English motorway network in strip map form. One of the earliest cartographic models, strip-mapping lends itself particularly well to this application. Colour is used to designate road types, and each map indicates services, service areas, interchanges and the next major town. *Design: Automobile Association, U.K.*

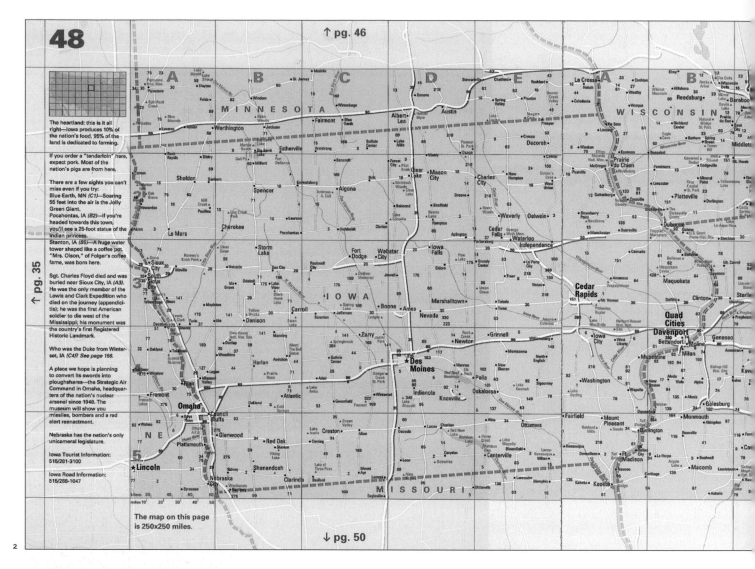

The heartland: this is it all right—Iowa produces 10% of the nation's food. 95% of the land is dedicated to farming.

If you order a "tenderloin" here, expect pork. Most of the nation's pigs are from here.

There are a few sights you can't miss even if you try:
Blue Earth, MN (C1)—Soaring 55 feet into the air is the Jolly Green Giant.
Pocahontas, IA (B2)—If you're headed towards this town, you'll see a 25-foot statue of the Indian princess.

Stanton, IA (B5)—A huge water tower shaped like a coffee pot, "Mrs. Olson," of Folger's coffee fame, was born here.

Sgt. Charles Floyd died and was buried near Sioux City, IA (A3). He was the only member of the Lewis and Clark Expedition who died on the journey (appendicitis); he was the first American soldier to die west of the Mississippi; his monument was the country's first Registered Historic Landmark.

Who was the Duke from Winterset, IA (C4)? See page 156.

A place we hope is planning to convert its swords into ploughshares—the Strategic Air Command in Omaha, headquarters of the nation's nuclear arsenal since 1948. The museum will show you missiles, bombers and a red alert reenactment.

Nebraska has the nation's only unicameral legislature.

Iowa Tourist Information:
515/281-3100

Iowa Road Information:
515/288-1047

The map on this page is 250×250 miles.

← pg. 35

↓ pg. 50

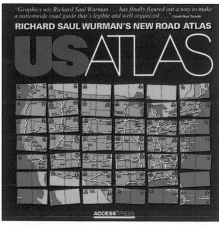

**1 – 4**

*USAtlas*

Richard Saul Wurman's road atlas of the United States was the culmination of a series of map publications that began with *Cities*, which presented same-scale comparisons of old and new cities, and continued with *Urban Atlas*, the first comparative statistical atlas of major American cities (1967).

Wurman went on to publish the well-known *Access* guides, which revolutionized the travel guidebook. The impulse for these guides, Wurman has explained, was his own 1980 move to Los Angeles, where he experienced 'a full state of disorientation. *LA Access* was organized primarily by location – a simple desire

to know where one was and what was nearby.' *USAtlas* developed when Wurman moved to New York and had difficulty using local maps of different scales. The atlas incorporates several features from earlier books and is based on a fifty-mile page grid, each segment taking approximately one hour to

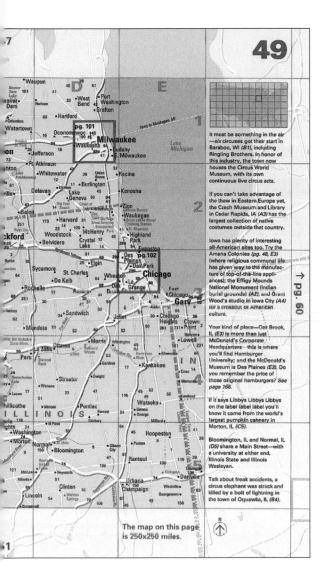

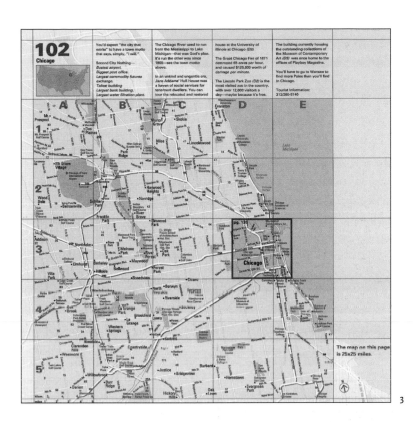

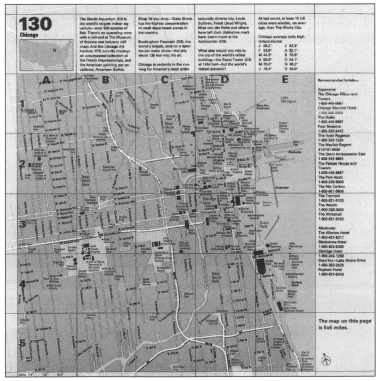

drive. Related maps, which are colour-coded to indicate their relationships to the main maps and their respective scales, zoom in or out of the main map to show scales of 25 × 25 miles or 5 × 5 miles [3–4]. The concept is admirably carried out within the limitations of a printed book, and the spreads include annotations and useful information in the margins, a device drawn from the *Access* guides. A more recent series of guides presents a selection of towns as a mini-version of *USAtlas*, with a grid of ten minutes' walking time per page. *Design: Richard Saul Wurman, U.S.A.*

1 – 4
**Upside-down Map**

This cartographic concept evolved in response to the shortcomings of traditional maps, particulary in motoring situations. As in the Pen DOT map designed by Joel Katz (p. 152 [1]), the typography is orientated towards the direction of travel. Otherwise, the map uses traditional cartographic conventions. Having become frustrated with publishers who, it seemed to him, were failing to understand the significance of his design, John Sims decided to publish it himself. The map has since found its place in the market.
*Design: John Sims, U.K.*

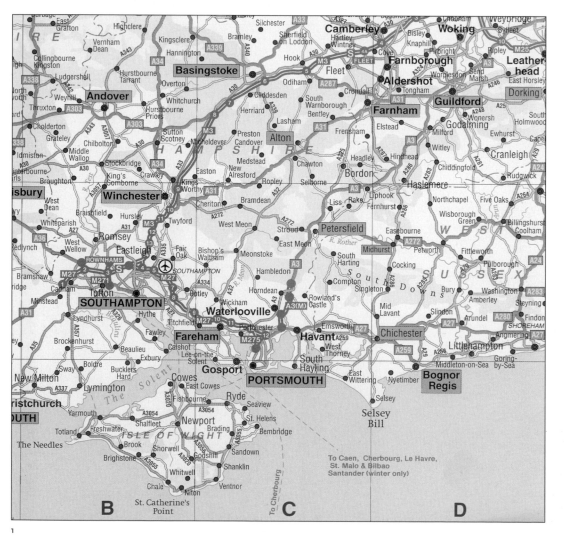

1

2

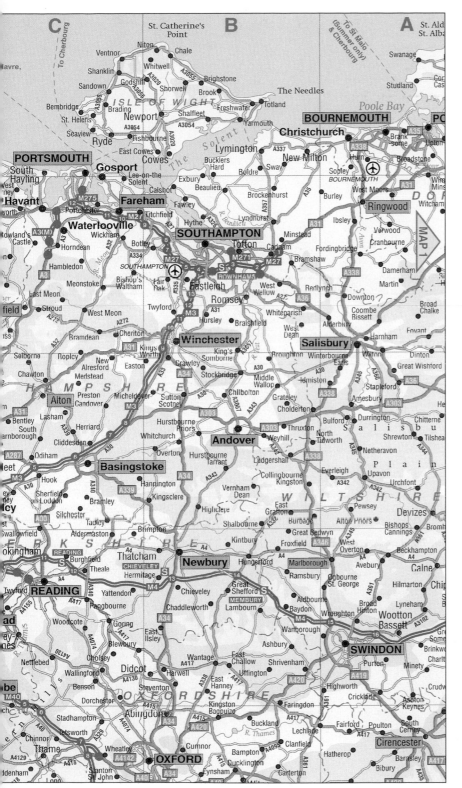

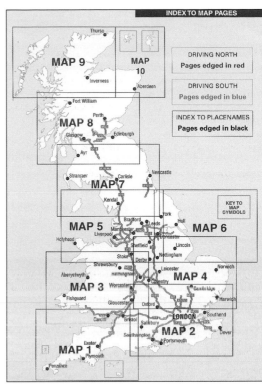

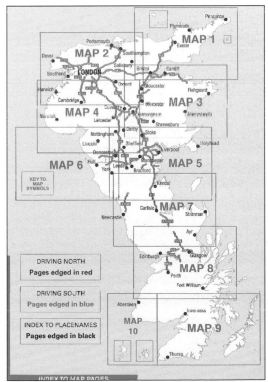

1

**Mobile Phone Coverage Map**

The extent of service coverage
is an important selection
criterion for potential mobile
phone users. In the highly
competitive u.k. mobile
phone market, coverage maps
are a vital element of the
marketing communications
portfolio. One 2 One
produces a range of coverage
maps targeted at different
audiences and varying in size
from A5 leaflets, such as the
Spring 1998 version pictured
here, to A2 large-scale
regional maps and A1 national
posters. Coverage data, which
is derived from a proprietary
computer-based cell planning
tool, is also made available as
an overlay for route-planning
software packages.
*Courtesy One 2 One, u.k.*

High quality outdoor coverage now.
Variable quality outdoor coverage now.
Planned service, end of Spring 1998.
Planned service.

**one 2 one**

1

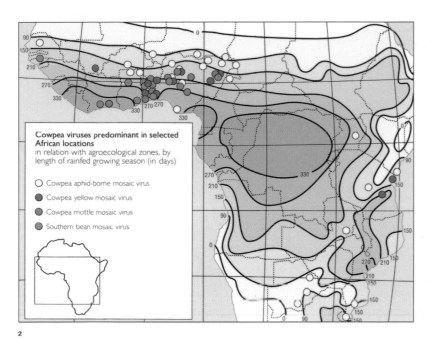

**2**

**2**

**Distribution of Cowpea Virus**

On this map for an annual report showing the distribution of types of virus affecting the cowpea plant in areas of tropical Africa, the coloured circles show locations against the backdrop of the growing season, the clusters demonstrating the vulnerability of certain selected areas of mid-range growing conditions. By also including country boundaries, it is possible to see which countries are most affected.
*Design: Trevor Bounford, U.K.; client: International Institute of Tropical Agriculture*

**3**

**Distribution of Cassava Mealybug**

The extent of distribution of the cassava mealybug pest within tropical Africa, and of the release sites of its parisitic enemy, are shown. The map also shows the general distribution of the pest-controlling parasite and specific locations where its establishment or otherwise has been recorded. Numbers help identify which parasite has been most effective.
*Design: Trevor Bounford, U.K.; client: International Institute of Tropical Agriculture*

Within the legend of image 1:

Cowpea viruses predominant in selected African locations
in relation with agroecological zones, by length of rainfed growing season (in days)

○ Cowpea aphid-borne mosaic virus
● Cowpea yellow mosaic virus
● Cowpea mottle mosaic virus
● Southern bean mosaic virus

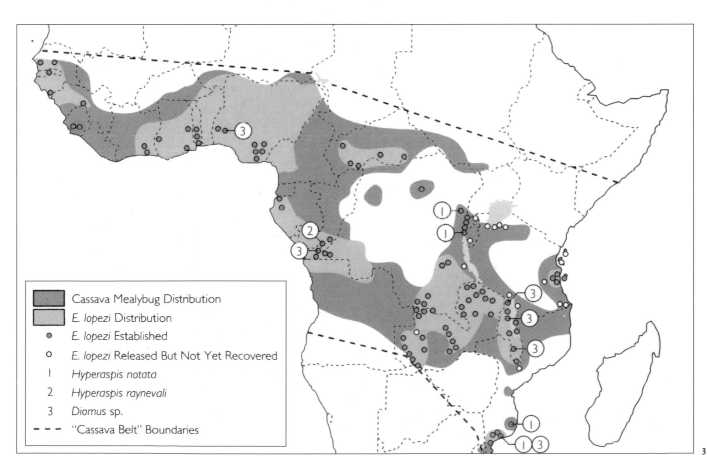

Cassava Mealybug Distribution
E. lopezi Distribution
● E. lopezi Established
○ E. lopezi Released But Not Yet Recovered
1 *Hyperaspis notata*
2 *Hyperaspis raynevali*
3 *Diomus* sp.
– – – "Cassava Belt" Boundaries

**3**

# The Language Map of Africa
## Clarifying Multiple Types of Information

Work on the language map of Africa dates from the 1970s. The major design challenge involved in making the new map [1] was to bring together information from a number of different national compilations and to solve the frequent inconsistencies. The current priority is to establish a system for the collation of new material.

David Dalby's *Language Map of Africa* is the first part of the world-wide Linguasphere project designed to record all of the languages and linguistic communities on the planet. The *Language Map* is an integral part of a programme which poses important questions regarding the integration of different types of information within a single computerized system.

The Linguasphere Observatory, a transnational research institute based in Wales, France and India,

is collaborating with UNESCO's Linguapax programme in the preparation of a seamless geographical information system (GIS) map of the world's languages and linguistic communities. This endeavour is based on the notion that the world's languages, whatever their relative importance, together provide the linguistic framework (linguasphere) around which a multilingual continuum of human communication and creativity (logosphere) has been constructed since the beginnings of humankind. Although the frontiers between individual languages are more fluid than has frequently been supposed, the organization of data on tens of thousands of languages and dialects requires a stable and clear-cut system of referential classification. This has been provided by Dr Dalby's recently completed *Linguasphere Register of the World's Languages and Linguistic Communities*, in which a detailed classification is presented as a network of almost eight hundred sets of closely related languages and dialects (or isolated languages) within a framework of ten referential sectors and a hundred referential zones. The emphasis is on close and readily observable relationships amongst modern languages rather than on hypotheses about their possible prehistoric origins.

The *Language Map of Africa*, coloured and coded according to the sectors, zones and sets of the *Linguasphere Register*, presents an overview of the detailed groupings of almost 2,500 African languages and will be extended in two directions, using the facilities provided by the MapInfo system of computerized GIS cartography:

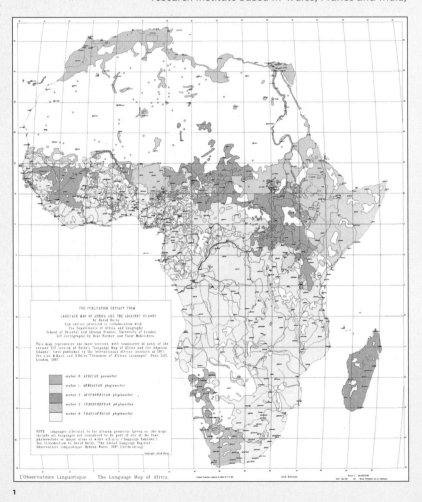

L'Observatoire Linguistique   The Language Map of Africa.

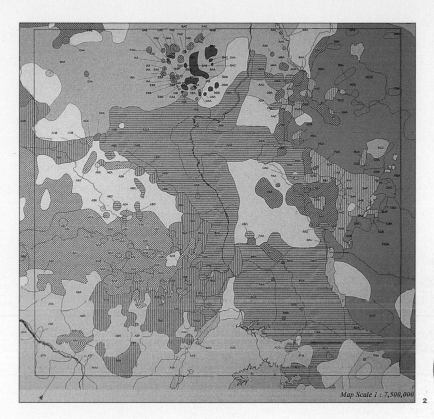

Map Scale 1 : 7,500,000

2

- vertically within Africa, by zooming into enlargements of the linguistic detail in each area of that continent, with the option of viewing computerized overlays presenting parallel data on physical features, demography, education, etc. (including the latest information on the recent effects of war and famine);

- horizontally into Europe and Asia, by extending the same system of reference and cartographic presentation to the languages of those continents, with an initial concentration on the complex linguistic geography of South Asia (including the latest information on endangered minorities).

Apart from the many linguistic, geographical, technical and financial problems posed by this global undertaking, the question of information design is also of major importance. At the heart of the undertaking is a transnational web site (www.linguasphere.com) which will serve as a focal point for communications on the global work of the Linguasphere Observatory and on the different aspects of this global programme. It is hoped to develop an integrated design for the web site, for the language maps and for the presentation of textual data, and to create an interest in this endeavour amongst specialists in information and graphic design.

The design aspect of this programme also relates directly to the question of writing systems, which are a parallel concern of the Linguasphere Observatory. Apart from the design and presentation of Asian and other major scripts (the Linguasphere web site will be available in Hindi and other languages, as well as in English and French), work has already been undertaken in Africa with UNESCO support to develop and apply a two-layered Latin alphabet. By making available two contrasting forms of each Roman letter, this extended alphabet provides a sufficient choice of characters for the phonemic transcription of virtually any language in the world (including a standard set of superscript accents for the indication of tone) and can also be readily employed for the transliteration of other alphabetic or syllabic scripts.          *David Dalby*

2
_____

A detail from the complete map. The apparent simplicity of parts is somewhat misleading. Linguistic complexity is found throughout Africa south of the Sahara, but is less easily portrayed cartographically in cases like the Bantu languages, where their close relationship (represented in yellow) masks great internal variation.

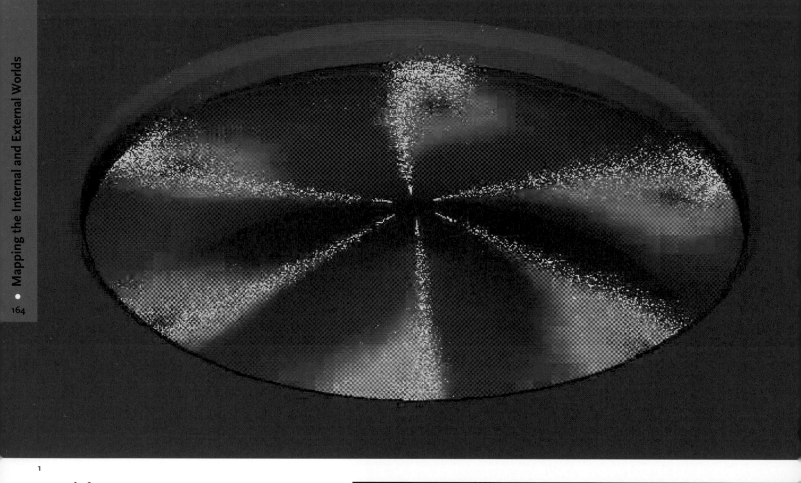

1

## 1 – 3
**Internal Combustion Engine**

In their quest for improved engine performance and lower emissions, scientists in Daimler-Benz's Cybernetics and Simulation Research Department are using advanced computer techniques to 'look' at the internal combustion processes of engines. Events which take a fraction of a second in real time can be viewed in slow motion on a monitor and studied in great detail. [1] is a simulation of the mixture formation in a diesel engine; it shows the decay of the nozzle jet inputs into small droplets (seen at the centre of the image as small yellow dots). Exposed to high pressure and a hot environment, the droplets vaporize into the yellowish streaking along the jet axes. [2–3] show the simulation of two injector nozzles in a spark-ignition engine set at different jet-cone angles into the cylinder head; [3] shows a superior mixture which produces less soot and nitrogen oxide emissions.

2

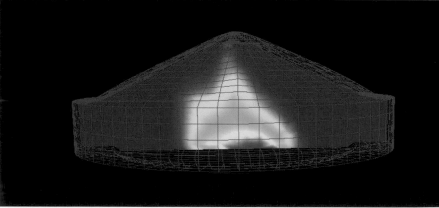

3

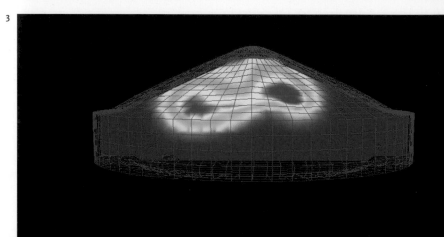

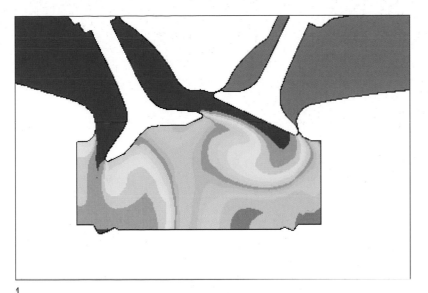

1

[4] shows how the flame in a spark-ignition engine spreads within the gas mixture and how the air-fuel mix (red) combines with the residual gas (blue), while [5] illustrates a simulated flow field. *Computer simulation: Helmut Gildein and Dr Frank Otto; courtesy Daimler-Benz HighTech Report, Germany*

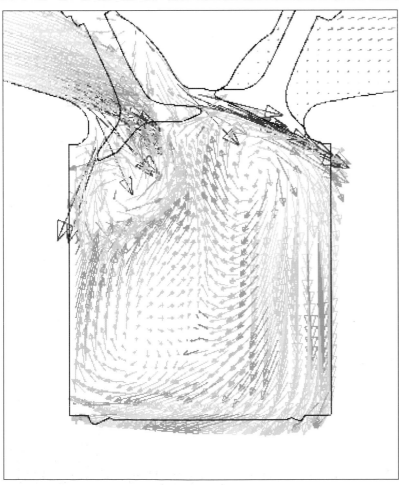

5

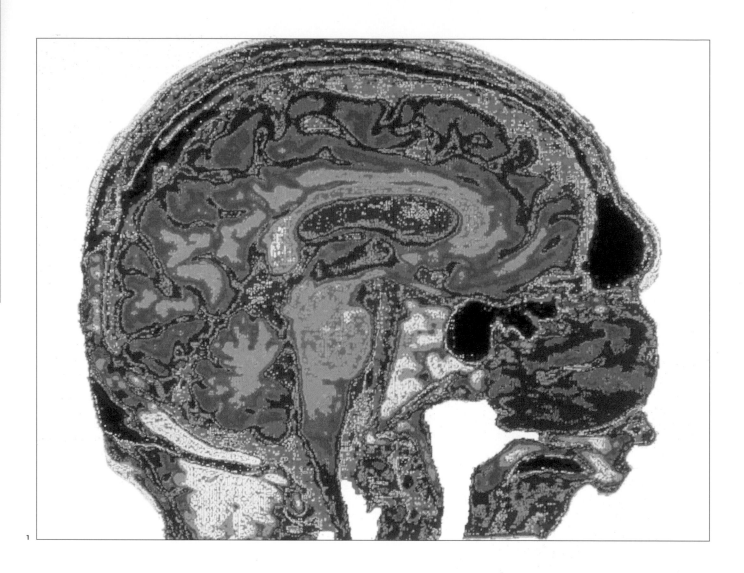

1

**Brain Imaging**

The mapping of the human body is sometimes referred to as anatomic cartography, a not inappropriate term since map makers have always had to rely on exploration and patient measurement.
In a similar way, the inner living body was inaccessible to visual observation until x-rays were invented in 1895. Since then, a wide range of imaging techniques have been developed capable of recording almost all aspects of the internal body from two-dimensional cross-sections to fully modelled three-dimensional forms. Each scanning technology provides a different type of information and degree of resolution. Like conventional maps, different projections reveal different interpretations of the same region. As in early terrestrial maps, colours are for the most part arbitrary.

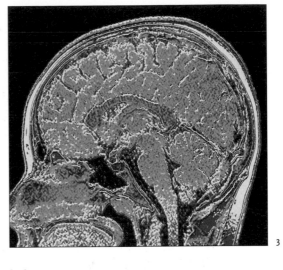

3

2 – 3
Brain Imaging

Brain images may be created
by means of computerized
axial tomography (CT) and
magnetic resonance imaging
(MRI). [1] is a false-colour
MRI of the head and normal
brain of an eighty-year-old
man. [3] also shows a healthy
brain by means of colour-
computed tomography. [2]
is a false-colour MRI of a
mid-sagittal section through
a human head; it shows
the structures of a normal
brain, airways and
facial tissues.
*Photos. Courtesy Science Photo
Library, London*

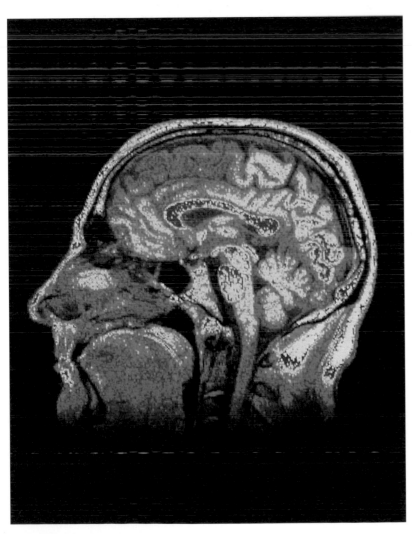

2

# Notes

**Electronic In-Car Navigation Aid** *(pages 38–39):*
*Software:* Rice Brothers; *information graphics*
*team:* Gill Scott & Associates: Gill Scott, Mark
Annison, Liz Orna, Hilary Whelan.

---

**Rolls Royce Aerospace** CD-ROM *(pages 70–73):*
The cinegram was designed by Detlev Fischer as
part of his Ph.D. programme at Coventry University.
See D. Fischer, 'A Theory of Presentation and Its
Implication for the Design of Online Technical
Documentation', Ph.D. thesis, Coventry University.
The development and potential of the cinegram is also
reported in a number of papers, including C. J. Richards
and D. Fischer, 'Cinegrams: Interactive Animated Systems
Diagrams for Technical Documentation', in *The Use of IT
in Art and Design, Technical Report* 26 (Loughborough:
Advisory Group for Computer Graphics) (1994);
D. Fischer and C. J. Richards, 'The Presentation of
Time in Interactive Animated Systems Diagrams',
in R. A. Earnshaw and J. A. Vince (eds), *Multimedia
Systems and Applications* (London: Academic Press, 1995),
pp. 141–59. The partners in the OMIMO project were:
Coventry University, U.K.; Etnoteam, Italy; VTT
Information Technology, Finland; Caplan, Germany;
and Rolls Royce plc, U.K. Prof. Clive Richards is the
founder and director of the Visual and Information
Design (ViDe) Research Centre in the Coventry School
of Art and Design at Coventry University, U.K.
More about the Centre can be found at the
URL=http://.www.csad.coventry.ac.uk/vide/

---

**Air Traffic Control Screens** *(pages  92–95):*
Illustrations 1–6 are reprinted from L. Reynolds, 'Colour
for Air Traffic Control Displays', *Displays* 15 (1994),

pp. 215–25, with kind permission from Elsevier Science –
Amsterdam, The Netherlands.

---

**SUI's and GUI's** *(pages 97–101):*
IDEO is one of the world's largest product
design development companies and has been
responsible for over two thousand complex medical,
computer telecommunications, industrial and consumer
products. It has led the way in the relatively new discipline
of interaction design and has pioneered techniques for
improving the user/product relationship. IDEO's
philosophy is that the technology should not drive the
product, but instead the user-centred design process
must drive the technology to achieve a successful
and usable end solution. From roots in London,
IDEO now has offices in London, Milan, Boston,
Chicago, San Francisco, Palo Alto and Tokyo.

*References:*
Black, A., and Buur, J. 'GUIs and SUIs: More of the
    Same or Something Different?' In Anzai, Y., Ogawa, K.,
    and Mori, H. (eds), *Symbiosis of Human and Artifact*
    (North Holland: Elsevier, 1995), pp. 187–92.
Black, A., Bayley, O., Burns, C., Kuuluvainen, I.,
    and Stoddard, J. 'Keeping Viewers in the Picture:
    Real-world Usability Procedures in the Development
    of a Television Control Interface'. *CHI '94 Conference
    Companion* (New York: ACM, 1994), pp. 243–44.
Burns, C., Dishman, E., Verplank, W., and Lassiter, B.
    'Actors, Hairdos and Videotape – Informance
    Design'. *CHI'94 Conference Companion*
    (New York: ACM, 1994), pp. 119–20.
Buur, J., and Windum, J. *MMI Design – Man Machine
    Interface* (Copenhagen: Danish Design Centre, 1994).
Gentner, D. R., and Grudin, J., 'Why Good Engineers

(Sometimes) Create Bad Interfaces'. *CHI'90 Conference Proceedings* (New York: ACM, 1990), pp. 277–82.

Gould, J.D., and Lewis, C. 'Designing for Usability: Key Principles and What Designers Think'. *Communications of the ACM* 28 (1985), pp. 300–11.

Grudin, J. 'Systematic Sources of Suboptimal Interface Design in Large Product Development Organisations'. *Human-Computer Interaction* 6 (1991), pp. 147–96.

Harada, A., and Tamon, H. 'Simulating Mental Images through User Operation'. *Industrial Design* 157 (1992).

March, A. 'Usability: The New Dimension'. *Harvard Business Review* (September/October 1994), pp. 144–49.

Mulligan, R. M., Altom, M. W., and Simkin, D.K. 'User Interface Design in the Trenches: Some Tips on Shooting from the Hip'. *CHI 91 Proceedings* (New York: ACM, 1991), pp. 232–36.

Nayak, N. P., Mrazek, D., and Smith, D. R., 'Analyzing and Communicating Usability Data'. *SigCHI Bulletin* 27/1 (1995), pp. 22–30.

Nussbaum, B., and Neff, R. 'I Can't Work this Thing!' *Business Week* (29 April 1991), pp. 58–66.

Oviatt, S. 'Interface Techniques for Minimizing Disfluent Input to Spoken Language Systems'. *CHI'94 Proceedings* (1994), pp. 205–10.

Sakamura, K. *TRON Human-Machine Interface Specifications* (Tokyo: TRON, 1993).

Sato, K. 'User Interface Design Theory: Special Feature: Cutting Edge on Interface Design'. *Industrial Design* 157 (1992).

Suchman, L. *Plans and Situated Actions* (Cambridge: Cambridge University Press, 1989).

Verplank, W. 'Sketching Metaphors: Graphic Invention and User-interface Design'. *Friend 21: International Symposium on Next Generation Human Interface* (Japan, 1991).

**A National Park Multimedia Program**

*(pages 108–11)*

*Design:* GRID (Group for Information Design), Switzerland; *concept:* Hans Kren; *mentors:* Urs Graf, Michael Renner; *contributors:* Klaus Robin, Director, National Park, Zerneg/Graubünden; Martin Heller, Britta Allgöwer, Geographic Institute, Zurich University; *screen text:* Hans Lozza.

**Neighbourhood Maps for the Blind** *(pages 140–43):*

For more information about this project, see Jens Bernsen (ed.), *Finding the Way by Ear, Hand and Foot* (Denmark: Danish Design Centre, 1996).

*Concept and project management:* Danish Design Centre; *tactile maps:* Damsgaard & Lange, Carl Bro Informatik; *Sirius Navigator:* Contrapunkt A/S, Carl Bro Informatik; *paving stones:* Knud Holscher; *industrial design,* Charlotte Skibsted.

**The Language map of Africa** *(pages 162 63):*

Further information on all aspects of this programme, including copies of the *Linguasphere Register*, may be obtained from Observatoire Linguistique, Hebron, Dyfed SA34 0XT, Wales, or by e-mail from zoe@linguasphere.com.

# Suggestions for Further Reading

Aicher, Otl. *Analogue and Digital*.
    Germany: Ernst und Sohn, 1992

Brand, Stewart. *The Media Lab*.
    U.K.: Penguin Books, 1987.

Future Books, 1–4 Adprint. U.K., 1946.

*Graphic Communication through Isotype*.
    U.K.: University of Reading, 1980.

Hall, Stephen. *Mapping the Next Millennium*.
    U.S.A.: Vintage, 1993.

Haller, Rudolf, and Kinross, Robin. *Otto Neurath*,
    vol. 3: *Gesammelte bildpädagogische Schriften*.
    Austria: Hölder-Pichler-Tempsky, 1991.

*Information Design Journal* 6/1 (1990).

Hogben, L. T. *From Cave Painting to Comic Strip*,
    'A kaleidoscope of human communications'.
    U.K.: Parrish, 1949.

Johnson, Norman, and Kotz, Samuel.
    *Leading Personalities in Statistical Sciences*.
    U.S.A.: John Wiley and Sons Inc, 1997.

Kirkham, Pat. *Charles and Ray Eames, Designers of the
    Twentieth Century*. U.S.A.: MIT Press, 1995.

Mijksenaar, Paul. *Visual Function:
    An Introduction to Information Design*.
    The Netherlands: 010 Publishers, 1997.

Museum für Gestaltung Zurich, *User Instructions*.
    Schriftenreihe 16. Switzerland, 1993.

Neurath, Otto. *International Picture Language*.
    U.K.: University of Reading, 1980.
—. *Modern Man in the Making*. U.S.A.: Kopp, 1939.

Norman, Donald A. *Signals Are the
    Facial Expressions of Automobiles*.
    U.S.A.: Addison Wesley, 1992.

Schriver, Karen. *Dynamics in Document Design*.
    U.S.A.: Wiley, 1996.

Snyder, John. *Flattening the Earth*.
    U.S.A.: University of Chicago Press, 1993.

Stefoff, Rebecca. *Maps and Map Making*.
    U.K.: British Library, 1995.

Tufte, Edward R. *Envisioning Information*.
    U.S.A.: Graphics Press, 1990.
—. *The Visual Display of Quantitative Information*.
    U.S.A.: Graphics Press, 1983.
—. *Visual Explanations*.
    U.S.A.: Graphics Press, 1997.

Wurman, Richard Saul. *Follow the
    Yellow Brick Road*. U.K.: Bantam, 1992.
—. *Information Anxiety*.
    U.S.A.: Doubleday, 1989.
—. *Information Architects*.
    U.S.A.: Graphis Press, 1996.

# Index of Designers and Suppliers

**AA Multimedia**

Automobile Association Developments Limited

Fanum House

Basingstoke

Hampshire RG21 4EA

England

tel: +44 990 448 866

fax: +44 1256 491 974

**ai design**

Peter Burgeff

Lachnerstrasse 3

80639 Munich

Germany

tel: +49 89 169170

fax: +49 89 1679698

**Am+A** (Aaron Marcus and Associates)

1144 65th Street, Suite F

Emeryville, California 94608-1053

U.S.A.

tel: +1 510 601 0994

fax: +1 510 547 6125

email: Aaron@AMandA.com

[in New York]

Cogito Learning Media, Inc.

20 Exchange Place, 44th Floor

New York, New York 10005-3201

U.S.A.

tel: +1 212 220 8735

fax: +1 212 361 6342

email: Ed@AMandA.com

**Baumann & Baumann**

Taubentalstrasse 41

73525 Schwäbisch Gmünd

Germany

tel: +49 7171 92 79 90

fax: +49 7171 92 79 99

**Bertron & Schwarz**

Ulrich Schwarz

Wilhelmstrasse 19

73525 Schwäbisch Gmünd

Germany

tel: +49 7171 927 100

fax: +49 7171 927 1050

email: bertron.schwarz@projektnet.de

[in Berlin]

tel: +49 30 399 03 188

fax: +49 30 399 03 186

email: bertron.schwarz@projektnet.de

http://www.projektnet.de

**Bureau Mijksenaar**

Dreeftoren

Haaksbergweg 15

1101 BP Amsterdam Zuidoost

The Netherlands

tel: +31 20 691 4729

fax: +31 20 409 0244

email: mijks@euronet

**Chapman Bounford & Associates**

Trevor Bounford

115c Cleveland Street

London W1P 5PN

England

tel: +44 171 636 2554

fax: +44 171 580 0625

email: bounford@atlas.co.uk

**Daimler Benz A.G.**
Presse Forschung und Technik
Epplestrasse 225
70546 Stuttgart
Germany
tel: +49 711 17 0
fax: +49 711 17 2 22 44
http://www.daimler-benz.com

**Danish Design Centre**
Birgitta Capetillo
Vesterbrogade 1C
1620 Copenhagen V
Denmark
tel: +45 33 69 33 69
fax: +45 33 69 33 00
email: design@ddc.dk

**Diseño Shakespear**
Cuidad de La Paz 421
1426 Buenos Aires
Argentina
tel: +54 1 554 0188/0220
fax: +54 1 553 3582
email: info@shakespear-design.com

**Dorling Kindersley**
9 Henrietta Street
Covent Garden
London WC2E 8PS
England
tel: +44 171 836 5411
fax: +44 171 836 7570

**Dynamic Diagrams, Inc.**
12 Bassett Street
Providence, Rhode Island 02903
U.S.A.
tel +1 401 331 2014
fax +1 401 331 2015
email: lenk@DynamicDiagrams.com

**Edwards Churcher**
Rodney Edwards
34 Great Sutton Street
London EC1V DX0
England
tel: +44 171 490 5922
fax: +44 171 251 9474

**Felco S.A.**
2206 Les Geneveys-Coffrane
Switzerland
tel: +41 32 868 1466
fax: +41 32 857 1930

**Gill Scott & Associates**
48 Rochester Place
London NW1 9JX
England
tel: +44 171 267 7016
fax: +44 171 284 1556

**GK Graphics Incorporated**
Masahiko Kimura
2-19-16 Shimo-ochiai
Shinjuku-ku Tokyo
161-0033 Japan
tel: +81 3 3953 5653
fax: +81 3 3953 5654

**GRID** (Gruppe for Information Design)
Hans Kren
Centralbahnplatz 8
4051 Basel
Switzerland
tel: +41 61 272 90 50
fax: +41 61 272 90 51
email: kren@grid.ch

*Guardian* **Graphics**
Paddy Allen
*The Guardian*
119 Farringdon Road
London EC1R 3ER
England
tel: +44 171 278 2332
fax: +44 171 837 2114

**Henrion, Ludlow & Schmidt**
12 Hobart Place
London SW1 0HH
England
tel: +44 171 235 5466
fax: +44 171 235 8637
email: hp@hls-ci.demon.co.uk

**Hoffmann Stähli**
Centralbahnplatz 8
4051 Basel
Switzerland
tel: +41 61 272 90 50
fax: +41 61 272 90 51
email: hoffmann@datanetworks.ch

**IDEO**
Rosemary Lees
7 Jeffreys Place
Jeffreys Street
London NW1 9PP
England
tel: +44 171 485 1170
fax: +44 171 482 3970

**Information Design Unit**
Old Chantry Court
79 High Street
Newport Pagnell
Bucks MK16 8AB
England
tel: +44 1908 210 060
fax: +44 1908 210 571
email: enquiries@idu.co.uk

**Intégral**
14, rue kléber
93107 Montreuil-Paris
France
tel: +33 1 49 88 80 50
fax: +33 1 48 70 17 31

**Kognito Visuelle Gestaltung**
Alt Moabit 62/63
10555 Berlin
Germany
tel: +49 30 399 253 0
fax: +49 30 399 253 11
email: info@kognito.de

**The LEGO Group**
DK-7190 Billund
Denmark
tel: +45 75 33 11 88
fax: +45 75 35 33 60

**Linda Reynolds & Associates**
27 Spencer Road, Chiswick
London W4
England
tel/fax: +44 181 747 3293

**Luger Graphik**
Eponastrasse 7
6900 Bregenz
Austria
tel: +43 5574 45 55 00
fax: +43 5574 45 55 04
email: rluger@luger.vol.at

**Marine Gate Shiogama**
Shiogama-ko Kaihatsu
1-4-1 Minatomachi Shiogama-shi Miyagi
985-0016 Japan
tel: +81 22 361 1500
fax: +81 22 361 1471

**MetaDesign plus GmbH**
Uta König
Bergmanstrasse 102
10961 Berlin
Germany
tel: +49 30 69 579 233/200
fax: +49 30 69 579 222

**Miedaner, Burke, Hoffmann**
Hölderlinstrasse 40
70193 Stuttgart
Germany
tel: +49 711 299 8067
fax: +49 711 299 8067
email: bfg.mie.hoff.bur@z.zgs.de

**Minds Eye Design**
Francis Newman
The Old Church
Quicks Road, Wimbledon
London SW19 1EX
England
tel: +44 181 543 2211
fax: +44 181 543 7812
email: francis.newman@virgin.net

**Nordbok**
Gunnar Stenmar, President
P.O. Box 91
40232 Gothenburg
Sweden
tel: +46 31 171 885
fax: +46 31 132 842

**North Design Ltd**
Studio 405
Butlers Wharf Building
36 Shad Thames
London SE1 2YE
England
tel: +44 171 357 0071
fax: +44 171 490 4968
isdn: +44 171 357 0750

**Observatoire Linguistique**

Dr David Dalby

Hebron, Dyfed SA34 1XT

Wales

tel/fax: +44 1994 419 300

---

**Odermatt &Tissi**

Schipfe 45

8001 Zurich

Switzerland

tel/fax: +41 1 211 94 77

---

**One 2 One**

Elstree Tower

Elstree Way, Boreham Wood

Herts WO6 1DT

England

tel: +44 181 214 2121

fax: +44 181 214 3431

---

**Pocknell Studio**

David Pocknell

Readings

Blackmore End

Braintree

Essex CM7 4DH

England

tel: +44 1787 463 206

fax: +44 1787 462 122

---

**QA International**

329 rue de la Commune Ouest, 3rd floor

Montreal, Quebec

Canada H2Y 2E1

tel: + 1 514 499 3000

fax: +1 514 499 3010

**Richard Saul Wurman**

The Orchard

180 Narragansett Avenue

Newport, Rhode Island 02840

U.S.A.

tel: +1 401 848 2299

fax: +1 401 848 2599

email: wurman@ted.com

---

**Professor Clive Richards**

Design Research Centre

Coventry School of Art and Design

at Coventry University

Priory Street

Coventry CV1 5FB

England

tel: +44 1203 631 313

fax: +44 1203 838 667

---

**Scopo**

Güterstrasse 145

4053 Basel

Switzerland

tel: +41 61 363 25 10

fax: +41 61 363 25 30

email: contact@scopo.ch

---

**Sensorium**

Yoshiaki Nishimura

1-5-11-208 Daita

Setagaya-ku

Tokyo 155-0033

Japan

tel: +81 3 5433 7266

fax: +81 3 5433 7270

email: nish@kt.rim.or.jp

**Siemens Design & Messe GmbH**
ICE Team
Tölzerstrasse 2c
81379 Munich
Germany
Frank Zebner
tel: +49 89 6368 3475
Stephan Apetauer
fax: +49 89 4900 3245

**Studio Progettazione grafica**
Sabina Oberholzer, Ray Knobel, Renato Tagli
CH 6675 Cevio
Switzerland
tel/fax: +41 754 18 24
email:Soberhol@tinet.ch

**Tube Graphics**
6-199-40-204 Akasako, Minato
Tokyo 107
Japan
tel: +81 3 3505 4577
fax: +81 3 3588 6276
email: tube@3.rim.or.jp

**Uitgeverij Het Spectrum b.v.**
Postbus 2073
3500 GB Utrecht
The Netherlands
tel: +31 30 2650 650
fax: +31 30 2620 850

**The Upside Down Map Co Ltd**
John Sims
Suite 5, Derwent Court
Macklin Steet
Derby DE1 1SG
England
tel: +44 1332 369 090
fax: +44 1332 363 377

**Van der Meer**
Garden Cottage
18 Ditton Park Road
Datchet
Berkshire SL3 7JB
England
tel: +44 1753 540 708
fax: +44 1753 540 709
email: 101375.2156@compuserve.com

[in The Netherlands]
Ch. van Montpensierlaan 65
1181 RP Amselveen
The Netherlands
tel: +31 20 640 1670
fax: +31 20 445 0478
email: popup@PHPC.com